SELF, WORLD, AND TIME

Ethics as Theology 1

AN INDUCTION

Forthcoming:

FINDING AND SEEKING

Ethics as Theology 2

ENTERING INTO REST

Ethics as Theology 3

Self, World, and Time

• •

Ethics as Theology 1

AN INDUCTION

Oliver O'Donovan

WILLIAM B. EERDMANS PUBLISHING COMPANY
GRAND RAPIDS, MICHIGAN / CAMBRIDGE, U.K.

Published 2013 by
Wm. B. Eerdmans Publishing Co.
2140 Oak Industrial Drive N.E., Grand Rapids, Michigan 49505 /
P.O. Box 163, Cambridge CB3 9PU U.K.

Printed in the United States of America

19 18 17 16 15 14 13   7 6 5 4 3 2 1

Library of Congress Cataloging-in-Publication Data

O'Donovan, Oliver.
Self, world, and time / Oliver O'Donovan.
pages cm. — (Ethics as theology 1 an induction)
Includes bibliographical references and index.
ISBN 978-0-8028-6921-0 (pbk.: alk. paper)
1. Christian ethics.   I. Title.

BJ1251.O365   2013
241 — dc23
2013005017

www.eerdmans.com

Contents

Preface

And is there room for yet another turn around the floor with that "bad idea" (as it has been called by a contemporary with a gift for a phrase), Christian Ethics? If Christian Ethics has proved a bad idea, it must be in part because it has been too much the playground of good ideas. Fresh starts, new methods, programs for reconfiguration, new special foci, chase one another bewilderingly through the issues of its journals and the proceedings of its conferences — like the unveiling of the year's new cars at the annual auto show, though with less sense of familiarity. Twenty years ago Johannes Fischer complained that "in Protestant circles, at least, Theological Ethics has seemed in danger of disintegrating in a series of arbitrary new initiatives."[1] And perhaps it was always so. Some disapproving observations of one of those condescending philosophical pagans of the early fourth century paint a picture we can recognize all too well:[2]

> The Christian philosophy is said to be simple. Though it includes some teasing niceties about God, the sum of which preoccupation is a fairly uncontroversial claim of a creative cause — sovereign, original, and source of all that is — the greater part of its attention is given to moral instruction. Leaving to ethicists such harder questions as the nature of virtue and moral reason, the relation of morality to the passions and so

1. *Leben aus dem Geist: Zur Grundlegung christlicher Ethik* (Zürich: Theologischer Verlag, 1994), p. 15.
2. Alexander of Lycopolis, *On Manichaean Beliefs* (PG 18:412). Here and elsewhere throughout this volume, unless otherwise indicated, translations of ancient texts are my own.

on, its teachers ply the highways of edification, not proposing detailed guidance for acquiring each virtue in particular, but heaping one general exhortation on another unsystematically. To this the masses respond well, one may see, by growing more civilized and by imprinting their common morality with a stamp of piety, so that starting from the morality of custom thus fanned into flame there develops by small increments an appetite for the Good in its own right. Yet as their debates became more and more polarized over the years, more people became involved in contentious wrangling, which led to the emergence of those whom one might describe as the more energetic and argumentative at the head of rival schools. This compromised the hidden genius of their morality. As the prominent champions of the schools argued without precision, as the masses became ever more disturbed about the questions, as there was no standard and no norm for resolving the controversies, competitiveness took over, as so often happens, and left everything a total mess.

Too much a creature of fashion to be trustworthy as a science, too much a creature of ideas to be pastorally helpful to the church, too "soft" for the university, too "abstract" for the theological seminary, Christian Ethics finds itself a despised outcast in the world, always hunting round for protective alliances. When I began my studies forty years ago, it seemed that Moral Philosophy of the analytic school would be its tutelary genius. The Euthyphro dilemma would determine the scope of its appeal to authority; attention to deductive logic would help it "clean up its language." Today the struggle for its soul is fought out between the statistical columns of the social sciences and a dogmatic theology newly confident on Trinitarian or sacramental foundations. Absorbed on one side into the theological construction of reality, propelled on the other into the bureaucratic mapping of contemporary history, Christian Ethics is condemned, it would seem, to surrender gracefully to one or another imperial organization of reality, if it is not to defend a point that turns out to have no dimensions.

And yet we remember what Voltaire said of God: "si Dieu n'existait pas. . . ." The dimensionless point on which Christian Ethics sits is not a chimera. It is shared with the reasons and discourses of moral thought and moral teaching. Dimensionless, because it is a tipping-point, the moment at which reason becomes action, and of the solid realities that crowd it in on every side there are questions to be asked and answered that could not be posed from any other point than that. Practical reason cannot be projected onto the world-map of the scientific empires. Its outsider character speaks of its proximity to existence, to the questions people ask for themselves before they have been to college to learn what questions they ought to ask. There will have to be a Christian Ethics for as long as people ask what they are to do, how they are to live their lives, how their doing and their living may bring them closer to God or put them further from him. Their questions are not ideas, and they are not posed from any discipline. Ideas and disciplines are simply attempts to get grappling irons on them. The questions assert themselves, and keep on coming back when they seemed to be settled. Those who ask them will not be satisfied with being told that they are non-questions. The only point to be resolved is whether any help will be had with them from the faculties of learning in church or university — if (and it is a big "if") such faculties survive in either church or university. Shall the thoughtful be strengthened by a community of reflection? Or shall their questions be faced each time in ignorance that they have ever been faced before?

In case this line of defense should seem to be a rather complacent way of shielding a disorderly enterprise, let me add that there is much that those who pursue the discipline of Ethics can do to make good the promise of ordered intellectual help. Perhaps I may offer a pointer or two, *in usum peritiorum,* for those who will practice this discipline with me and after me. It may also serve as an apology for whatever may strike an unprepared reader of this book as merely idiosyncratic.

First, they must enter into the lived experience of practical deliberation for themselves, and inhabit it as residents, not as those visiting on occasional research trips. For myself, I now see that I embarked on Christian Ethics as I embarked on life and faith themselves, by being catapulted into it. It was a simple demand of existence that I should ask two questions: what I was put on earth to do, and what it could mean that I was put on earth to do it. Some will reproach me that if I had accepted a plain and straightforward answer to the first of these questions, I need never have bothered so much with the second. I would simply have got up from my desk and gone forth, like the early disciples, to preach the Gospel, feed the hungry, and heal the sick. Perhaps there is some truth in the reproach. I admire those who, once given their task, gird up their loins and go their way, saluting no one on the road. But stern activism is more attractive as a charism than as a universal prescription. Once the larger questions have presented themselves, they, too, impose a task which allows of no refusal.

They, too, are the "travail that God has given to the sons of man to be exercised therewith" (Eccles. 1:13).

Secondly, since Ethics is necessarily an architectural enterprise, bringing trains of thought together which have different inner logics, the practitioner must be able to function polymorphously, now telling a narrative, now mounting an argument that proceeds to valid inference, now depicting reality adequately from many sides. There is always a temptation to play Ethics as rugby is played: eying up the shortest route, putting the head down, shoving as hard as possible. We would do better to remember the old wisdom that every science must "save the appearances." The Ethics we inherit is something to make sense of, however critical our perspective on it. As a branch of theology it is not only speculative but also hermeneutic; it has its texts — canonical, traditional, and critical — and must attend to them. It may never say, "I have no need of that hypothesis!" — not, at least, until it has understood what need others have had for it, ensuring that none of its serviceability is lost. There is a scholarly task of careful and judicious remembering; Ethics no less than doctrine needs its *ressourcement.* That is one reason why moralists should not think themselves exempt from the normal rules of careful scholarship, using original sources and, where possible, original words, and not only from favorite and familiar authors, but from those who have been lost sight of or may seem of doubtful value. Yet as a branch of theology Christian Ethics must also answer for its concepts theologically. It cannot be merely eclectic, picking up from the tradition or beyond it whatever may take its fancy. It must have God's revelation on its mind, must think in reference to it and in obedience to the canonical Scriptures that attest it.

There is another intellectual challenge, which is the interpretation of the times. That "late modernity" in which we are given to live and act can never be taken as self-evident; it is a philosophical task in itself to understand it. There is a style of dealing with modernity all too knowingly. Modern "social conditions" are comprised, we are told, of individualism, egalitarianism, technology, and capitalist enterprise; these are the terms on which mankind today lives, and we must either acknowledge them sensibly or be doomed to be forever criticizing them nostalgically — end of discussion! Alas, it is the doom of modernity to be bound up in an over-simple knowingness about itself! Our own age is the hardest of all ages to understand. It is composed of a mass of popular ideas and perceptions, often difficult to document though they are as familiar as the air we breathe, which acknowledge no duty to be consistent with each other. They may be derived from the thoughts of great thinkers, but when they are, they have lost most of what subtlety and discrimination they once had. They ration and restrict our access to thought about life and action in ways we must look hard in order to recognize. (It is not easy to think in a disciplined way through any social question outside the constraints of a would-be economic calculus which scarcely deserves the serious philosophical name of "utilitarianism.") Even more cramping, they determine the way we describe the material objects of our thought, so that there are decent and gullible souls, for example, who think it "unscientific" to refer to the child in the womb as "a person." Sophistry treads hard, as it has always trodden, on the heels of Ethics, but never harder than in a world of intense and over-heated communications. The tramp of its boot must be heard before we can step to one side and free ourselves, recognizing where we have come and what decisions we must take. Such coming to recognition of our place and time is the condition for doing, or indeed being, anything.

All of which comes down to saying that academic practitioners of Christian Ethics must, no less than the active believers they presume to accompany and share their reflections with, be alert to their agency, to their world, and to their time. So we are launched on our theme, and it is best that we should simply look ahead to what may be expected from it. The book the reader now holds, whether in the elegance of a traditional bound and printed volume or in the hasty functionality of a Kindle, is announced as an "Induction," to pave the way for further "Explorations." It is concerned primarily with the form and matter of Christian Ethics as a discipline, in relation to its material (moral thought and moral teaching), its setting among the humanistic faculties of study, and its proper shape, a triadic trajectory in which self, world, and time are reflected and restored.

This trajectory will, I anticipate, supply the framework for the explorations to follow, provisionally called *Finding and Seeking,* which follows the agent's trajectory in search of a path of action, and *Entering into Rest,* which considers the ends-of-action to which the agent looks forward, the "ends" that can be reflected upon, where faith and hope are gathered into love, provisional and, to the extent that Ethics can speak of them without taking responsibility for what lies beyond its scope, ultimate.

I date the first intimations of this book to some hours spent in Canterbury Cathedral in early 2003, waiting for a ceremony to begin. I had equipped myself with the smallest volume on my shelves, one that would easily fit a pocket and arouse no suspicions on the security scanner. It was à Kempis's *The Imitation of Christ* in the old World's Classics format, a text that I normally find too disorderly and sentimental to trust myself to, but which, on this occasion, created a healthy disturbance in my mind. "The children of Israel in times past said unto Moses, 'Speak thou unto us, and we will hear: let not the Lord speak unto us, lest we die.' Not so, Lord, not so, I beseech thee, but rather with the prophet Samuel I humbly and earnestly entreat, 'Speak, Lord, for thy servant heareth'. Let not Moses speak unto me nor any of the prophets, but rather do thou speak. . . . They may indeed sound forth words, but they cannot give the Spirit."[3] So I was prompted to ask further about the gift of the Spirit and its implications for the forceful moral objectivism of my *Resurrection and Moral Order*. A "Pentecost and Moral Agency," perhaps?

To record my debts would be to record my biography since then. Let me simply state that the manuscript benefited greatly from detailed criticisms offered by my friends Bernd Wannenwetsch and John Hare, and, as always, by my dear wife, Joan Lockwood O'Donovan. The generous hospitality of the Centre for Apologetic Scholarship and Education at New College in Sydney, Australia, gave me a first opportunity to explore some of the terrain in September 2007, and an occasional reminiscence of that pleasant Australian visit still flavors the text. An opportunity to join a small group of colleagues in Rome in 2008 for a colloquium at the Accademia Alfonsiana to mark the tenth anniversary of Bernard Häring's death prompted some questions about the discipline, which have come to rest in Chapter Four, and an invitation to Montreal as the 2009 Birks Lecturer at McGill University allowed me to develop some further themes in the congenial context of a return to Canada. Finally, a colloquium mounted by the McDonald foundation at Cambridge in 2011 on Christian Ethics in the University gave me an occasion to share my reflections on the shape of the discipline with distinguished colleagues. I am bad at keeping track of what happens to words I have published once they get thrown back into the kneading-bowl, but I am reasonably sure that the editors and publishers of the following journals and volumes could recognize material they first exposed to daylight, for which I am very grateful: *Studies in Christian Ethics*, for "The Object of Theological Ethics," vol. 20 (2007): 203-14, "Prayer and Morality in the Sermon on the Mount," vol. 22 (2009): 21-33, and "The Future of Theological Ethics, vol. 25 (2012): 186-98; *Studia Moralia*, for "Interpreting the Theological Criteria of Moral Thinking," in *What am I Doing when I do Moral Theology?* (Supplemento 5, 2011); Peter

---

3. *De imitatio Christi*, trans. F.B. (Oxford: Oxford University Press, 1903, 1951), 3:2.

Candler and Conor Cunningham, for "Deliberation, Reflection and Responsibility" in *The Grandeur of Reason* (London: SCM Press, 2010). If I have missed any, I hope that may be ascribed to my incompetence, not to my ingratitude, though, as the reader who persists with the following pages will learn, incompetence is no excuse. I cannot omit a final word of appreciation to my collaborators at Wm. B. Eerdmans in Grand Rapids, and especially to the Vice President and Editor-in-Chief, Jon Pott. It is always a privilege to work on terms of old friendship with a publishing house that has served theological literature so intelligently for so long.

New College, Edinburgh
May 2012

CHAPTER 1

Moral Awareness

Unfamiliar trains of thought and specialized patterns of inquiry may be provided with an *introduction,* which show the student their grounds and scope. But what of trains of thought and patterns of inquiry, communications, and practices which have been with us since before we were even conscious of thinking? No introduction can be imagined for what we can never meet for the first time: conscious experience itself, in all its forms. And a very great part of conscious experience is our sense of ourselves as *agents.* Practical reasoning has been our native element. Yet we can, and may, feel the need to grow more aware of that element; we can learn to ask sharper questions about it and to open ourselves up to the logic of what we have always simply counted on. And we can ask about what it tells us of more ultimate things: of God, especially, who stands behind and before our agency, and of our position in his world and time. If we cannot pursue these questions, we cannot be at rest with ourselves; but if we can pursue them, we can be helped and encouraged to do them. It is with that in view that we propose this *induction* into Ethics as Theology, to be followed in due time, if God permits, by a further *exploration* of it.

Introduction

"So then we are debtors," says Saint Paul quite suddenly in the middle of everything (Rom. 8:12). Certainly, we are debtors! We know it as soon as we are told it. We swim in a sea of moral obligations, tangled in seaweed on every side, acknowledging claims here, asserting responsibilities there. It is

1

our native element. Yet we have no idea how it became so. What led Saint Paul to his "so then" was a long account of what God had done for us: justification by free grace, one righteous act that gave life to many, delivery from the power of law. But at every moment it assumes that we were debtors already: debtors when we suppressed the truth in ungodliness, debtors when we were reconciled to God, debtors when we could not continue in sin that grace might abound. Of this or that concrete debt we can explain how it came about: we signed a rental contract, agreed terms of employment, made a confession of love. But these acts were not the start of our indebtedness. We rented the flat because we had a job we had to get to each morning; we took the job because we needed to be near our girlfriend; even the confession of love was shaped by a complex of obligations shaped by emotional exchanges that gained ground on us and closed us in. Obligations formed us, and we formed obligations, for as long as we ever knew ourselves. They governed our behavior and shaped our character before we knew how to think of them. We did not *reach* our thoughts of obligation by inference from other thoughts, abstract ideas like those of mathematics or aesthetics or immediate perceptions of the senses. What other thoughts could there have been that could have immersed us in this sea of obligations for the very first time?

Let us say, we *awake* to our moral experience in the beginning. What seems like the beginning is not really a beginning at all. We wake to find things going on, and ourselves going on in the midst of them. The beginning is simply the dawning of our consciousness, our coming-to to what is already happening and to how we are already placed. For some thinkers about Ethics, both academic and popular, this has proved an embarrassment. They would like to find a safe ground of knowledge of ourselves or of our situation, some truth drawn from a scheme of objective knowledge — theology, sociology, evolutionary biology, or whatever — and to work from that point to discover *whether there is* such a thing as a morality, and *what it is*. "Morality should be governed by science!" is the familiar hunting-halloo of the revisionary theorist. It would be nice to test the ground of morality before we step on it. But to all such proposals there is one inevitable reply: they come too late. *Already* we are asking questions about our actions and obligations. *Already* we are contesting the reasons for acting in this way or in that way. The scientific starting-point, whatever it may have been, is far behind us and beyond our field of vision. It is a reasonable ambition, of course, to situate moral awareness within the wider scheme of things, to identify its presuppositions and its function in the world, but one must begin with it where it is to be found, which is where we find ourselves, active subjects caught up in the middle of things. Here is the element of truth in the ancient and recurrent claim that value cannot be derived from fact. The medieval mystics held that love, the employment of the will, arises "without previous knowledge"; twentieth-century philosophers denied that "is" could imply "ought."[1] A great deal of confusion has surrounded this claim, which is frequently mistaken for a license for voluntarisms and intuitionisms that reduce moral reasoning to nonsense. But we must grant the starting-point: moral experience is not constructed or achieved out of non-moral experience; it is woken up to as experience that has accompanied other experience, present from the beginning and distinct in kind.

And what is this distinct kind? If we follow Paul's exposition further, we find that indebtedness accompanies *phronēma*, which is to say, practical thought, thought about what we are to do. Practical thought is the most commonplace of human rational exercises, for action is the first and elementary horizon of human existence. At home in our minds like fauna in their native habitat, reasons for acting need no introduction to us but occupy their mental environment with assured right of possession. We can hardly think of thinking without thinking first of them. The moment of pure observation, when our practical impulses come to rest in sheer wonder at our object, when we stand right back behind the line of sight: that is the rare and acquired moment of thought, the one that we need some kind of introduction to.

When we speak of "morality," then, we do not speak of *what we do*, but of *how we think what we are to do*, which is to say, how we *act*. Doing is something that humans have in common with non-human animals: birds build nests, mammals hunt for food. But morality involves taking note of doing, making doing the object of thought, not simply by looking back at it afterwards, but by looking forward to it as a project. Whether morality can be attributed to non-human animals is a speculative question; we have no discourse with them, and cannot exchange narratives of action, so that we do not know what a dog *thinks it is doing* when it chases a ball. Narrative is an important condition for moral thought. Homer is of interest to Ethics because he narrates the deeds of Achilles and Hector and shows us what makes them great from their motives to their accomplishment. Yet

---

1. Jean Gerson, *Opusculum* 1: *"Stat amorem naturalem causari sine previa cognitione in re que diligit, amat vel appetit."*

narrative is not itself moral thought. Homer's Achilles is simply Achilles, his Hector simply Hector. If as we read we say, "As were Achilles and Hector, so are we!" moral thought has taken over from narrative. It arises at the tipping-point between narrative and self-awareness. We can own, or we can deny, that we, too, like Hector and Achilles, are actors. To deny it, we need only curl up with a book and become literary critics, historians, or sociobiologists. The motives which Homer attributes to Hector and Achilles need not be motives for us. But if we do not deny our agency, we experience their motives as a kind of demand laid on us. And finding ourselves awake, we know we must give our attention to being wider awake. Out of this focused attention moral thinking arises.

Morality supposes life of a certain kind, life of intelligence, responsibility, and freedom which is, as Saint Paul has told us, the life of "Spirit." Even to pose a moral question is already to tread water, to trust our weight upon the element of Spirit. Is it, then, Spirit that lays our obligation upon us, to which, in the last resort, we are indebted? Paul gives the impression of being about to say just that: "we are debtors not to the flesh but . . . ," and our minds supply the conclusion. But Paul steps deftly aside and postpones that conclusion until some prior understandings are in place. We have no independent standing over against Spirit; Spirit is not one among our creditors whom we can look in the eye and ask how much we owe him. What we "owe" Spirit is precisely that we owe anyone anything; we owe Spirit our moral obligations. So when he reaches the conclusion it is not a matter of being debtors to Spirit; it is *being led by* Spirit.

The prior understanding Paul puts in place is the danger of a mistake, and on a grand scale: "We are debtors, not to the flesh. . . ." From the moment we first find ourselves immersed in moral experience a *false* apprehension of obligation may arise, a practical reason grounded not in Spirit but in "flesh," *phronēma sarkos,* as Saint Paul calls it. Moral intelligence, with its sense of obligation, responsibility, and freedom *vis à vis* reality, can be mislocated, falsely framed within a material set of presuppositions, improvised around bare factual determinants. We may think of the bombastic "imperative of research" which drives the proud biotechnical Leviathan, or of the empty pleadings of politicians urging us to be "led into the future" (as though we could go anywhere else!). There are moral discourses without foundations, and we may pile up a crushing burden of debt, a fearful sense of the doom that hangs upon our actions, and yet find no space for Spirit. It is self-destructive to say "ought" of the heavy, necessitous "is" of dull factual realities; it plunges us into the self-refutation ly-

4

ing in wait for all materialism, which is to understand that there is, after all, no understanding. It puts to death the life of freedom Spirit has conferred. Life in Spirit, on the other hand, is a different kind of "putting to death," for it deflates purely material necessities and asserts freedom against them. It annuls every sense of being "debtors" to the flesh.

In what direction, then, does our debt lie, if not to Spirit and not to flesh? The first step towards an answer is given in the word "life." We are in some sense debtors to the business of living, but that means there is a difference between *being alive* and *living*, between the life we live without trying to do so and the life we must *reach out* to live, by knowing ourselves not merely materially conditioned but spiritual: "If by the Spirit you put to death the body, you shall live." Human beings cannot live as vegetables, which grow, leaf, and flower simply by virtue of being alive. They must appropriate life, make it their own. We make a difference between "life," as such, and "a life" which has to be lived for ourselves. And, the apostle proceeds, to live by Spirit is also to be led by Spirit. The spiritual life is a *directed* life. In giving life to our mortal bodies, in constituting us as subjects of moral experience, Spirit "leads" in the direction of free action. Which brings the apostle to a third designation: "Spirit himself bears witness to our spirit" (8:16). Induction into life and action is accomplished by a word of truth addressed to us, a declaration of the way things are between the world and ourselves. We are debtors to a life, a direction, and a truth.

And then we are in a position to add, debtors also to God. For the witness from Spirit to spirit, Paul would have us understand, is a word from God to man. It originates beyond our human ken, yet is also a word from Spirit to spirit. The spirits are not equal; one is Creator, the other creature. Yet they are spirits together in a graced analogy; God's witness comes to one whom God has made to answer and reflect him. The spirit hearing is like the Spirit heard, though at the same time wholly unlike. That likeness is what being led by Spirit consists in, living a life that is given by Spirit and corresponds to Spirit's life. The witness tells us we are children of God, not tools, not subordinate implements moved around to serve purposes of which we know neither the why nor the wherefore, not random creatures of cosmic energy blown about as dynamics of flesh may chance to dictate. We address God as "Abba! Father!" — freed in this elemental prayer to affirm his works and make them our own. We are led to know ourselves for what we are, to come to ourselves in coming to our Father, to enact our existence truly. It is the freedom to live, the most total expression of active, conscious, authentically engaged existence. Any other life that may seem possible to live, any life conceived according to "the flesh," in terms of mere facticity, is not life at all, but a shadow-life that leads towards death.

Waking

The metaphor we have reached for, the metaphor of waking, speaks of a general, not of a specifically religious experience. "Man, yes, man outside the biblical revelation, awakes," wrote Balthasar.[2] Yet we have not been able to elaborate and explore it without theological concepts. It is a metaphor which makes a definite proposal about how general moral experience is to be understood, and that proposal is of Christian provenance. There are other metaphors in current use for what we do when we engage in moral thought. Some like to speak of "constructing" morality, comparing it to a building operation. Others conceive it as a variety of sight, speaking of "moral vision," or as a supplementary sense, a "feeling" of good and evil. Others again describe it as a crisis of bewilderment, talking of "resolving dilemmas," or as a state of indeterminacy where we "make choices." We need not refuse the illumination shed by any of these. For most purposes we can afford to be free with our metaphors, switching from one to another as the poetry of the moment or the play of light may suggest. But metaphors harden into categories, and it makes a difference in the longer term which we think of as foundational.

A purely philosophical justification can be given for the metaphor of waking, complete with its entailment of Spirit and hint of the presence of God. It is the task of moral philosophy to account for moral experience efficiently, equipping it with ordered concepts that clarify its logic and open it to critical discussion. To this work of conceptual ordering Christian theology has its own contribution to add, arising from its hermeneutic responsibilities to its canonical text. Philosophy is not as such text-based, though it may read philosophical texts and learn from them; its task is to render an account of reality, and in doing so it will take its concepts where it finds them. Theology, avoiding philosophy's hazardous smash-and-grab tactics, insists on having its primary concepts issued and duly signed for out of the scriptural inventory. Yet the difference between them may not be

---

2. Hans Urs von Balthasar, "Neun Sätze zur christlichen Ethik," in Joseph Ratzinger et al., *Prinzipien Christlicher Moral* (Einsiedeln: Johannes Verlag, 1975), p. 86: *"Der (außerbiblische) Mensch erwacht zum theoretisch-praktischen Selbstbewußtsein."*

as great as this metaphor may suggest, for since text alone can justify or falsify its own interpretation, the deployment of scriptural categories, too, has a hypothetical character, and in making this or that biblical concept central to its thought, moral theology runs its own risk that a rereading of the text may put its conceptual order in question. Nevertheless, the validity of a concept depends for theology not only on whether it seems to fit experience, but on whether it illuminates, and is illuminated by, the scriptural text. And that is as true for moral theology as for any other.

Theology has a further task over and above that of conceptual ordering, which takes it beyond the scope of philosophy. A theological justification for the metaphor of waking will show how it leads moral experience back to its source in God's purposes. It will account for experience in the light of what is told us of its causes and ends; it will situate it in the narrative of a God who, having made us as agents, now redeems and perfects us. Theology has a special interest in the *renewing* of human agency. It has to tell of conversion, and of how our occasional moments of moral wakefulness may lead into an awakening that will be complete and final: "Awake, sleeper, rise from the dead, and Christ shall shine upon you!" (Eph. 5:14).

Throughout the Scriptures of Old and New Testaments the cry, "Awake!" summons agents, human or divine, to exert themselves. In the poetic literature of the Hebrew Scriptures the exertion may be military, judicial, artistic, or even, addressed to the gentler breezes, erotic (Cant. 4:16). The early Song of Deborah (Judges 5:12) uses this cry to summon its heroine to military leadership; much later Deutero-Isaiah uses it to summon the city of Jerusalem to assume her proper dignity at the end of the exile (Isa. 52:1). The Isaianic apocalyptist echoes him (Isa. 26:19), calling on the city's inhabitants to rise from the dust and sing. Singing, especially, is a task that demands some wakefulness; a Psalmist launching a celebratory composition may call not only on his own inspiration but on his instruments, too, to wake (Ps. 57:8 = 108:1f.) The nameless Servant Prophet of Deutero-Isaiah, meanwhile, can speak of God's "awakening his ear" to prepare him to instruct others (Isa. 50:4). But most characteristically the cry is addressed to God himself, calling him to judgment, sometimes military, sometimes purely judicial. He will awake to vindicate an outraged poet (Ps. 7:6; 35:23) and to punish nations that have oppressed Israel (Ps. 44:23; 59:5). His "arm" will awake to repeat the drama of the Exodus (Isa. 51:9), and in Trito-Zechariah, most strikingly, God calls his own sword to awake, putting an end to royal authority in Judah (Zech. 13:7).

At this point the contrast between the Old Testament and the New could hardly be more striking. Nowhere in the New Testament do the faithful call on God to awake. God has already awakened, has already acted. All that remains now is for *them* to be awakened. But the call for human waking is not an indeterminate call for general mobilization, but has certain specific features. Twice in the Epistles (Rom. 13:11; Eph. 5:14) it rounds off a passage of moral instruction with a call for radical conversion. These two texts, while still talking about sleep, use a distinctive Greek verb, *egeirō*, with a rather wider meaning that is something like "get up." Its use here is no doubt encouraged by the Gospel narratives of Jesus' healing miracles. The specific sense of the more usual verb, *grēgorō*, is "to stay awake." Addressed to believers, it stresses the need for continual alertness: "Be awake! Stand firm!" (1 Cor. 16:13), especially applied to persistence in prayer (Col. 4:2) or to the vigilance of ministers (Acts 20:31). Twice the verb *nēphō*, "to be sober," is used alongside it: "Let us not sleep, but be wakeful and sober!" (1 Thess. 5:6); "Be sober, be wakeful!" (1 Pet. 5:8). Besides these two verbs for waking there is a third with a slightly different nuance again, *agrupnō*, meaning "to lose sleep" over something, applied, again, to conscientious ministry (Heb. 13:17) and to persistent prayer (Eph. 6:18).[3]

Two settings in the synoptic Gospels find the command of wakefulness on Jesus' own lips. One is the so-called "synoptic apocalypse," where it occurs in two brief parables — the one of the returning traveler who has left orders for the gate-keeper to stay up for him (Mark 13:34; Luke 12:37), the other of the householder who would not have gone to bed if he had known the thief's intentions (Matt. 24:43; Luke 12:39) — and also occurs in a saying used in conjunction with these: "Stay awake, for you do not know when . . ." (Mark 13:33, 35; Matt. 24:42; 25:13). Sometimes it is reduced to the single word, "Be awake!" (Mark 13:37; Luke 21:36). The second setting is the Gethsemane narrative, where Jesus commands his disciples to wait while he prays alone, and on returning rebukes them for falling asleep (Mark 14:34-38; Matt. 26:38-42): "Be awake and pray!" At this point it is impossible to draw a clear line between the literal and metaphorical senses of "waking." The disciples' literal sleepiness is a symbol of the spiritual danger against which Jesus warns them. When he adds "that you may not enter into temptation," these words are not attached

---

3. It is, of course, unwise to press lexicographical variations too hard, for the meaning of a word is not reducible to a mathematical point, and fashions of rhetoric erode boundaries. We find γρηγορῶ and ἀγρυπνῶ used interchangeably in the synoptic Gospels (cf. Mark 13:33 with 13:35 and Matt. 24:42, and cf. Mark 13:37 with Luke 21:36).

only to "pray!" but also to "be awake!" In this context even literal wakefulness is part and parcel of moral alertness.[4]

These synoptic uses lie behind two calls to wakefulness in the Apocalypse (Rev. 3:2-3; 16:15), both on the lips of the risen Jesus and both referring directly to the parables from the synoptic apocalypse. Here the two parables have been conflated: the thief who will come in the night and the Lord who will return in the night are now one and the same, and are, in fact, Jesus himself, who says, "I will come as a thief." Also from the synoptic context are the words about not knowing the time. The blending of these synoptic elements gives a new force to the metaphor. Ignorance of the moment and thief-like suddenness of the Lord's return are, for John, not merely the universal conditions within which faithfulness must be exercised; they are God's judgment on unfaithfulness. It is the *unwakeful* servant who will encounter the Lord as a thief and who will not know the moment of his coming. A new illustrative feature develops this thought: one who stays awake will have clean clothes ready to meet his master (3:4) and will not be caught in an indecent state (16:15).

And so the command to wake is addressed in the New Testament chiefly to the church, which ought to be able to count, if any agent could, on being awake already. It sets the church in a moment of crisis, put on the spot, by relating the achieved past to the future of Christ's coming and to the immediate future of attention and action. Wakefulness is anything but a settled state, something we may presume on, as we can usually presume we are awake as we go about our business. It brings us sharply back to the task in hand, the deed to be performed, the life to be lived. Waking is thrust on us. We do not consider it, attempt it and then perhaps achieve it; we are claimed for it, seized by it. That is why it is not just one metaphor among many for moral experience, but stands guard over the birth of a renewed moral responsibility.

World, Self, and Time

To what, then, must we wake? To what give our fullest attention? Our first glance picked out three moments from Saint Paul's exposition: we wake to

---

4. And so the later devotional tradition understood it — as, for example, in Bach's *St. Matthew Passion,* where Picander's text has *"Ich will bei meinem Jesu wachen, so schlafen unsre Sünden ein. . . ."*

life, we wake to its *direction,* and we awake to the *truth* that makes it possible. Now we attempt to unfold these three moments more schematically, beginning with the third.

(a) To be awake is to be aware of *the truth of a world.* When we say "world," there are many things we may mean, but we must at least mean this: our existence is framed within an order of things that stands behind and before it. The world was a reality before I was a reality, an object of attention to God, angels, and men before it was an object of my attention. It will, in all probability, persist after I am gone. To that order of things as it was and will be I have no direct access. I know the world directly only as I stand within it, calling it "my world." My world is around me, interacts with me, conditions me and responds to me. Yet my world is not a different world from the one that was before me and shall be after me. My world is bounded past and future by a world which was not and will not be mine, which did not and will not surround me, interact with me, condition and respond to me. This paradoxical constitution of "mine" in relation to "not mine" is what we mean by the world's *objective truth.* Objective truth is the condition of all moral awareness, for moral awareness is the demand that the world lays on my inner self without *being* my inner self. To be morally awake is to be "invested" or "taken over" by reality from beyond myself.

It is possible, we may suppose, to drift through the world half-attentive, asking it no questions and telling it no lies, treating it as a screen on which we can project ourselves, careless of its independent logic, careless of the distinctions that give it size and scope and the connections that give it coherence, never troubling to think about its order as a whole or in its parts. It is possible to attend to the world momentarily and in fragments, now to this aspect and now to that, without pulling these moments of attention together. It is not a matter of course that we shall attend to the world at all. It is there without our constructing it; it determines our fate whether we attend to it or not. We bump into it and knock up against it without ever actually having to imagine it. Yet if we are to be more than idle window-shoppers on the world's high street, we shall have to direct our attention upon it. We shall have to reckon not only with the fact that there is a world, but with what the world is like, where it has come from, where it is going, and how it holds together. These are not questions that answer themselves. Much moral thought, much conscientious doubt turns on how the various elements that constitute the world are properly conceived and described. Is human nature a playground of selfish genes or the lord of creation? Is the human embryo a child or a mere piece of tissue? Is our behavior conditioned, or is it chosen? Such descriptive questions are the stuff of moral debate; they determine all our practical attitudes.

It has often been suggested that moral (or practical) reason is distinguished by the fact that it is *prescriptive*, while theoretical (or speculative) reason is *descriptive*. That is certainly not right. Moral reason has a vast stake in description. It describes particular things, describes their relations and purposes, describes the way the world as a whole fits together. Without this descriptive exercise practical reason would not be reason at all. It cannot be that "reason is the slave of the passions."[5] That is to say, it cannot be that practical reason begins with a simple impulse, an undetermined will, which then calls on knowledge of what is true and false, independently arrived at, to shape the execution of its project. For the impulse on its own, apart from any rational description, can have no clear project. It cannot be the impulse it is — fear, desire, sympathy, or anything else — unless it knows something about the world from the start: there are things that pose a danger to existence, there is good that offers it fulfillment, there are fellow-beings whose case is like mine. World-description belongs, as they say, "on the ground-floor" of practical reason. There can be no prescription without it; neither can there be description which is neutral in its prescriptive implications. Only because this is so, can we think our way through the world practically.

But how can we learn to describe the world? A very simple answer suggests itself: we are sites of experience, and experience uniquely controls our understanding of how things are. What our eyes have seen and what our ears have heard is insurmountable evidence. Yet this very simple answer has always had a large difficulty to overcome. If the evidence of experience is insurmountable, it is also insurmountably subjective. It is confined to what each of us registers directly within his or her own sensory field, which is not only limited in content and perspective, but ontologically unresolved, open to various interpretations. "I saw a fish suspended over the altar as the priest celebrated the Eucharist!" No doubt you did. But *was* there a fish suspended over the altar? That question cannot even be asked until we move beyond the immediacy of first experience.

A dweller in the northern hemisphere, never having visited Australia, has no direct experiential ground for believing in that island-continent's existence, yet persists in believing in it, and with very good reason. We trust

5. David Hume, *Treatise of Human Nature*, 2.3.3, ed. L. A. Selby-Bigge (Oxford: Oxford University Press, 1888), p. 415.

the capacity of cultural traditions (some more than others) to assemble and interpret many experiences of reality. Those community-constructed interpretations that we know generically as "science" play a large part in that negotiation. Scientific doctrines may sensibly be called "empirical," just as water drawn from the tap in the Thames Valley region of England may be called "urine." It is a correct description of their *origin,* but in each case what we actually consume has been subject to very careful processing. The history of modern Western philosophy is caught in a perpetual love-hate relation with the data of experience, a cycle in which claims to its unique self-evidencing force are first proclaimed loudly and then, unobtrusively but decisively, negotiated down. Precisely because we know the world is objective, we know that the processing of experience by community criticism and tradition is needed. We know there are more things in heaven and earth than we can experience ourselves, and that what we experience ourselves is unintelligible to us till we are given tools with which to grasp it. We need traditional matrices to understand the fish we see over the altar or the sudden onset of pains in the chest. The self-evidencing certainty of experience does not underwrite these matrices. As the history of science continually shows, they can frequently be contested.

How, then, shall our readings of the world, derived from others' experiences as well as our own, be assessed? We stand in need of a critical measure — not to answer every question about the world straight off, but to provide us with a direction for intelligent questioning. And this is not merely a philosophical requirement, but a matter of practical urgency. Without a key to the world's meanings we shall never be able to sift through the complex of information we receive about, and through, the world, and bring it to some kind of order. "How shall a young man guard his way from corruption? By taking heed to it according to your word" (Ps. 119:9). Practical reason looks for a word, a word that makes attention to the world intelligible, a word that will maintain the coherence and intelligence of the world as it finds its way through it, a word of God.

(b) But practical reason's *way through the world* is, at the same time, *our way.* To be wakeful is to attend to *oneself.* If attentiveness means bringing the world into view, it means bringing ourselves into view together with the world. We can imagine abstractly what it might be like to observe the world without attending to ourselves, simply looking *in on* the world, as it were, as through a window. Such an abstraction forms the ideal horizon of experimental scientific method, which is founded on a discipline of self-abnegation on the part of the observer. But a discipline of self-abnegation

presupposes attention to oneself. Even experimental discipline has to be constructed by careful attention to the observer's persistent presence in the world. That presence, together with its perspective on what it sees, must be allowed and corrected for in the design of an experiment, simply because it is a fact of which the world cannot be rid. To attend to one's own presence in the world means becoming aware of one's point of view, identifying oneself as occupying an observation-point and recognizing that one's point of observation is only one such possible point. And since attention is not mere passivity but an active turning towards an object, to be aware of oneself as attentive is to be aware of oneself as active, to know that one is no mere creature of impersonal forces, but a site of initiative.

The summons to wakefulness is therefore a summons to attend to my agency. I find myself in the world, attending to it, taking initiatives in respect of it, responsible for those initiatives. I find myself a distinct agent, one among many, not universally responsible for everything that happens but for some things that happen in particular. And this distinct agent, I find, is precisely what *I am,* so that what I am responsible *for* shapes what is to become of me, for good or ill. I find myself poised between the saving and the losing of my soul. The summons to wakefulness confronts me with the menacing possibility of failure to realize myself: "Awake! Keep hold of your clothes!"

Before I first reflected on myself, there existed one whom God created when he created me, one who occupied the place I occupy. This creature existed in my mother's womb, and in its existence I existed. "My frame was not hidden from thee, when I was made in secret" (Ps. 139:16). But though God knew of my existence then, I did not. Even when my first observations of the world were granted to me, knowledge of my self lagged behind them. This observer that I am was in the world before I learned to call it "me." (Robert Spaemann likes to point out how small children speak of themselves in the third person before they learn to use the first.)[6] In adult life something like the state of worldlessness and selflessness recurs under sedation, in a coma, or when asleep; and so may the state of selflessness *without* worldlessness, as when I am so absorbed in an object of attention that I forget myself or, more disturbingly, when I suffer loss of memory and have to struggle to pick up the threads of my identity. Perhaps some pathologies like autism or gender-dysphoria can be understood as an unusual difficulty in grasping oneself. Of that, though, I have no special com-

---

6. Robert Spaemann, *Persons* (Oxford: Oxford University Press, 2006), p. 14.

petence to judge, and it is not these liminal phenomena of *incapacity* to attend to oneself that concern us now, but the more common *moral failure* to attend to oneself. Gene Outka has written of a duty "to honour our agential powers," a failure in which he connects perceptively with the vice traditionally named among the deadly sins as "sloth."[7] Depression, when we withdraw from agency and gaze out on the world with emotionless eyes, may present us with the phenomenon of sloth in an acute and overwhelming form. In the apocalyptic visions of the Old and New Testaments there are those who, in their flight from self-awareness, cry to the hills "Fall on us!" Yet that flight is not always despairing; it is sometimes careless. We may be half-aware of ourselves, inattentive to what we are and do, casting ourselves as passive victims of others' action rather than as centers of initiative. In a flurry of disorganization I drop and break some fragile object, turn in exasperation to my nearest and dearest and cry, "Now look what you have made me do!"

David Hume understood very well the importance of the mind's moment of attention to the self. Though never forming a view of personal identity stronger than Locke's notion of it as a sequence of memories, Hume assigned pride of place in his treatment of the passions to two forms of direct self-awareness, "pride" and "humility" (by which he meant something like our "humiliation").[8] Other-directed affections lay downstream of these, he thought, involving the transfer of pleasure and pain by sympathy, while the pleasure of pride and the pain of humility are directed wholly to the self. With this begins Hume's account of desire and action as essentially passive, so passive, indeed, that it ends in a denial of the freedom of the will. "The mind can never exert itself in any action which we may not comprehend under the term of perception," and it was through perception, and specifically through the perception of pleasure and pain, that Hume hoped to convert passive impressions into some kind of "active principle."[9] But on these terms it could be no more than a *re*-active principle. He overlooked the fact that self-reflection is *already* active, that the self we discover in the world is an agent *before* we discover it, acting on the world already, even in the very act of reflective self-awareness through which we catch sight of it.

---

7. Gene Outka, "Faith," in *The Oxford Handbook of Theological Ethics*, ed. Gilbert Meilaender and William Werpehowski (Oxford: Oxford University Press, 2005), pp. 279-82.

8. *Treatise*, 2.1.2, pp. 217-19.

9. *Treatise*, 3.1.1, p. 456.

(c) To wake is to become aware, in the third place, of *time*. World and
self are co-present only in the moment of time which is open to us for action.

"How shall a young man guard his way from corruption?" It is in the
person of a *young* man that the poet frames his question, adopting the
point of view of someone standing on the threshold of life, representative
of all who awake to the task of living. Time lies before him as his way
through the world lies before him; time and world are co-involved, so that
as he approaches the one he approaches the other. Time lies behind him
too, but of that he need say nothing, since what interests him is how to begin. Time before him is not determined, as time behind him is determined.
There is no history of his future written in some book of predictions. And
such a predicted or imagined future would be of no interest to him at this
moment, as he is engaged in deliberation as to how to guard his way from
corruption. The future that concerns him has no narrative; it has as yet no
depth or extension; it comes right up to the margin of his present, like water lapping at the quayside. This is the *immediate* future, future time in its
aspect of immediate proximity to the present. But what is the present? It
may be thought of as *outside* time, whether, as Augustine conceived it, the
eternal, the native element of God, or, as in a train of thought Jean-Yves
Lacoste has opened up, as the native element of feeling, prior to any thinking or acting; it may be thought of as a privileged moment *within* time, a
point of view upon time, looking back and forth across it. One way or the
other, what the present cannot be is a *period of* time, with dimensions and
extension. As soon as we sandwich it in between past and future, it disap-
pears into nothingness. It is fleeting, an indeterminable moment of transition of what-is-not-yet to what-is-over-and-done-with. We find ourselves
like salmon leaping in the stream, the present being our point of purchase
on our upstream journey, *disposing of* the past and *appropriating* the future. Constituted, in Heidegger's expression, by its "horizons," the points
at which past and future meet in interface, our hold on the present is simply a moment of coming together and opening up, when what we *have*
been faces what we *may* be.

The opening of the present is to the future, but not equally to the
whole of the future but to the future immediately before us, the *next moment* into which we may venture our living and acting, the moment which
presents itself as a possibility. There are vast tracts of time past, and quite
possibly of time future, which lie open to our speculation and imagination; there are ways of experiencing the present which shut out the horizons of past and future and concentrate wholly on the passing moment.

But the only time of *practical* immediacy is this future moment offered to present wakefulness. It is a future moment because we must still act into it; it is not realized yet. But in a sense it is also present, because it is now, before we act, that we confront it and may deliberate about it.

And because we may deliberate about it, we are unquestionably responsible for it. Of no other moment in time but this future-present moment is that true. There are other futures than this immediate future, each with its own ontic status. There is the future that *will in fact transpire* in days to come, which our successors will look back upon as their past time. To this future, high in ontic density though it may be, we have no epistemic access — ordinarily, let us add, since we need not rule out occasional manifestations of prophetic prediction. There is another future quite different from it, which is the future we imagine, prompted by fears or hopes or lazy presumptions of regularity. Such projected futures are easy enough to construct in imagination, but ontologically they are shallow; they make little claim on our belief — even though they often market themselves at astonishingly high prices! Then there is the absolute future, the future that winds up future, present and past in the appearing of Christ and the judgment of God on history. This has the ontic status of a promise, and is partially accessible to knowledge as the promise is heard and believed. Our responsibility is not for any of these futures, real or imaginary, any more than it is for the past. We do not attend to these futures, any more than we attend to the past, *deliberatively.* I reflect, but cannot deliberate, on what I ought to have done last week. I imagine, but cannot deliberate about what my life will be like many years hence.[10] I may hope for, but cannot plan to bring about, the coming of the Kingdom of God. Reflection on things remembered, anticipation of things projected, feed and shape my actual deliberations, for prudence, the virtue proper to deliberation,

---

10. A fine passage on deliberation in Aristotle's *Nicomachean Ethics* was taken up into Christian reflection by the Greek fathers. Here is what Maximus Confessor made of it (*Ad Marinum,* PG 91, 16f.): "We deliberate about what lies with us, is encompassed by our agency, and indeterminate in its outcome. The object of deliberation is possible action. We do not deliberate about wisdom, which has its own objective reality, nor about God, nor about events that happen necessarily and regularly like the revolutions of the seasons, nor about temporal events which succeed one another in predictable ways like the rising and setting of the sun, nor even about events which, though not uniform, are subject to natural probabilities like the greying of the hair at sixty or the growth of the beard at twenty, nor about naturally unpredictable and irregular events like storms and droughts and hail. All of that is meant by the phrase, 'what lies with us.'"

weighs up existing states and projectēd outcomes. But the focus of deliberation is not on these futures but on the immediate future, the forward-looking present, the future as it beckons to the present, the present as it opens to the future. To define this moment more precisely: it is the *available* future, the possibility that lies open to our action.

Does the Kingdom of God, then, not overshadow the available future and make it possible? Is the remote future merely "absolute"? Or does it, as in the first proclamation of Jesus, "draw near"? Certainly it draws near, and in that there lies the importance of *hope* to deliberation. But we must not think we can reach out and grab it. Our first thought must be to allow the horizon to be the horizon, to resist the temptation of taking over the ultimate and managing it. Practical reason is not a way of organizing the future. The public imagination has a nice way of making fools of moralists who are susceptible to flattery. It casts them in the portentous role of fortune-tellers and clairvoyants, tempts them, instead of advocating courses of action, to forecast the course of future events, and then dismisses them with a breezy, "They will never do it, though!" as though the whole business of morality lay in weighing probable outcomes. "I am no prophet, nor a prophet's son!" (Amos 7:14) is a motto for every moralist, professional and amateur. If we knew the story of the future hidden in God's foreknowledge, we should be beyond deliberation, beyond action, even beyond caring. "The kingdom of God is not coming with observation" (Luke 17:10). Even of the Son through whom God acts in history it is said that the day and the hour are not revealed to him. The price of agency is to know the future only indirectly, that we may venture on it as an open possibility. The future of prediction, dreary with anxiety or buoyant with hope, has to be held at bay, so that we may use this moment of time to do something, however modest, that is worthwhile and responsible, something to endure before the throne of judgment.

The Mishaps of Ethics

The major mishaps that befall moral experience all arise from failure of attention to one or other of the three objects to which we awake, the world, ourselves, and our moment of time. Ethics without reference to the *agent-self* becomes mere problem-solving; we see, or think we see, possibilities for sorting out the world's difficulties; we develop our programs for changing things without any sense of what it would mean for *us*, or for any possible "us," to act in that way. Perhaps we are persuaded that justice would be best served by reintroducing capital punishment or going to war? Very well, but what does it mean morally to be an executioner, a military commander, or a political leader in war? This form of moral degeneration, at home in the world of political opinions and administrative systems, is responsible for the various brands of "professional ethic," which envisage the agent simply as a functionary, not as a human being with a conscience to guard and a life to live. The lack of a reference to the *world*, in the second place, generates action that parts company with the conditions of nature, a busy "can-implies-must" morality, flexing its muscles energetically to overcome all obstacles but never stooping to pick something up from the ground. Here we meet the would-be "technological imperative," so well described by Jacques Ellul as making ends fit means rather than means ends. Thirdly, a morality may lack reference to the available moment of *time,* and so fail to concentrate upon what is fit to be done in this time and this place. Here we are on the terrain of idealism, which cannot bring reflection on actuality and possibility down from abstractions to the point where we actually find ourselves needing to act.

These two-legged tripods are genuine moral diseases, afflicting those who are used to taking life and action seriously. There are still more grotesque shapes lying across the pocked surface of ethical theory, one-legged tripods that could never take form in life but subsist only in the fantastic world of intellectual theory, from where they are lovingly transcribed into textbooks for the supposed educational benefit of the young: the consequentialism that entertains no standards but projected future outcomes; the motive-ethic which acknowledges no law but the formal laws of agency; natural-law realism with an exclusive interest in objective order. But good moral theory, like moral experience itself, triangulates.

And does the triangle of world, self, and time encompass everything relevant to moral experience? Not everything that lies within the view of *theoretical* reason, certainly, and if what theory can know, practical reason can act on, it does not encompass everything morality may need. Not God, not the laws of logic or mathematics or metaphysics. But we are seeking to trace the roots of *practical* reason, which is concerned with the living of our life within the world. Practical reason may turn its attention to these three poles without noticing whatever lies beyond them — and that is what people mean when they say they can be moral without being religious, or that they can be good without being intellectually complicated, which, in a limited sense, they can. We can run without knowing whether we are running due west; we can see without knowing whether we are looking at a cloud or a mountain; we can think without getting a purchase upon truth; we can also live, and think towards living, without answering the question what we live *for*. Yet, as the Psalmist said, our life is "beset behind and before" by God (Ps. 139:5), held in a magnetic field, as we might paraphrase it, by what lies beyond its purview. World, self, and time themselves melt into nothingness as we gaze on them intently; none of them is self-interpreting, but each has its coherence from something presumed, something that besets it behind and before. A wider wisdom is required if we are to hold *this* wisdom, the wisdom of morality, in its place: Christ the center of the world, the bridegroom of the self, the turning-point of past and future. And as we attend to how our thought may move among the three points of reference, we discover that there is nothing self-sustaining about that movement, nothing that we can simply manage on our own. Ethics opens up towards theology. As waking is the metaphor that stands guard over the birth of moral experience, being led by the Spirit stands guard over its expansion into moral thought, action, and reflection. And as we pursue this expansion we shall find ourselves coming back more than once, as in a spiral, to the triangulation out of which moral awareness arises. It is, after all, in the nature of an induction that it must always be revisiting familiar places and seeing them with new eyes.

At the level of pure awareness there is no fixed order in which world, self, and time come to consciousness. They are co-eventual. The world passes temporally and is thus patent to action; action is realized in world-engagement and thus in time; time is measured in action and so frames the objective world. Yet as practical thought moves *discursively* among them, correlating the one with the other, it has its own order, which is given by the goal of action. Practical thought is not speculative thought, which might envisage all three points of reference synoptically and with sustained attention, but, as the rational expression of our existence-towards-action, it has a journey to make which leads in a certain direction towards a certain end. There is, therefore, a discursive order, corresponding to this journey, which places each of these three moments in a sequence. Our next turn in the spiral, then, is to explore the steps of that journey by which the conscious subject moves through a determined world to an undetermined possibility in exercise of its freedom to realize possibility in the world by action.

CHAPTER 2

Moral Thinking

Reasonable Action

At the core of commonsense morality is the conviction that we must act reasonably. By this is meant more than one thing. It means that our actions must fit in with how things are, not fly in the face of objective reality. But it also means that we must think about what we propose to do in an ordered way. Simple awareness is not enough to ensure a reasonable judgment. When someone says, "Think what you are doing!" we are expected to give our minds to it, to harness our intuitions to a disciplined exercise of reason that will lead to a rightly formed resolution.

The commonsense conviction about acting reasonably has not gone unchallenged. Famously, the young David Hume argued against it. Reason, he thought, was receptivity to facts and relations of facts; its mistakes were due to ignorance of facts and relations, and therefore simple misfortunes. "I am more to be lamented than blam'd, if I am mistaken with regard to the influence of objects in producing pain or pleasure, or if I know not the proper means of satisfying my desires. No one can ever regard such errors as a defect in my moral character."[1] Here Hume tapped into a strand of radical voluntarism: what I know and don't know is simply my fate; I am responsible only for whether I have ill will or good will. In the earliest phase of medieval scholasticism Peter Abelard had proposed the shocking thesis that no one is guilty of sin who does not knowingly and deliberately defy God. No error of understanding, however grave, can

---

1. David Hume, *Treatise*, 3.1.1.

make an action culpable. Christ's persecutors, who knew not what they did, were free of blame.[2]

Aristotle had distinguished two types of rational thought, "the thought which knows and the thought which calculates."[3] "Theoretical" and "practical" reason are the names in common currency, though they were not Aristotle's own. We shall stick with them despite the disadvantage that the word "theory" has a narrower reference than "theoretical reason." Theoretical reason terminates not only in "theories" but in all kinds of assertion of truth, "x is the case." Practical reason terminates in an assertion of right, "y should be done." Yet the right and wrong of practical judgment, Aristotle insisted, correspond in some sense to the true and false of theoretical judgment: "What reason asserts, desire pursues. . . . The work of every rational function is truth, but that of practical reason corresponds to rightness of desire."

On how we understand this correspondence, much hangs. Did Aristotle intend no more than a *formal* analogy, judgments of right providing the conclusions of practical deliberations in the same way that judgments of truth provided the conclusions of theoretical inferences? Or did he mean something stronger, namely that the *content* of a valid judgment of right is *in accord with* a valid judgment of truth? Modern voluntarism followed the first interpretation: each type of judgment formed the conclusion of its own train of reasoning. Classical moral realism took the second, and there are two considerations that make this seem correct. In the first place, it brings Aristotle's distinction closer to a thought of Plato, who distinguished three powers of the soul, the rational, the propulsive, and the concupiscent, and argued that virtue consisted in a command of reason over the other two. In the second place Aristotle assigned a superior dignity to theoretical reason, which in its highest form was directed to the "most valuable" realities, while practical reason, or prudence, dealt with lower, changeable realities. But from this way of dividing the offices it follows that *theoria* could not be affectively indifferent. Practical reason had no monopoly on affection, as it later came to have in modern voluntarism.

The second reading of Aristotle was characteristic of the whole an-

2. Peter Abelard, *Ethics: Scito te ipsum*, ed. D. E. Luscombe (Oxford: Oxford University Press, 1971), pp. 54ff.

3. Aristotle, *Nicomachean Ethics*, 6.1139a. Hellenistic philosophy built on this dichotomy to posit two branches of study concerned with the operations of reason, τὰ φυσικά and τὰ ἠθικά, to which they added a third, τὰ λογικά, which had to do with speech and communication.

cient tradition more or less, not least the Christian branch of it. When Augustine divided reason into "contemplation," the unbroken absorption of the mind in highest reality, and "cogitation," a discursive, regulatory concern with material needs, he had no idea of a knowledge separated from will or affection. Contemplation had its own voluntative energy and emotion its own cognitive lucidity.[4] At the highest level "wisdom" perfected love, at the lowest cognition discerned between proper uses of relative goods. But it was an intellectual accident waiting to happen that the theoretical-practical division should become assimilated to the division between the cognitive and the affective powers of the soul, so that knowing came to be opposed to willing, affection autonomously free of knowledge.

This falling-out between, as is usually said, "fact" and "value" can claim to be at least as old as the European university, as we have indicated from Peter Abelard. Yet it is to the eighteenth century, especially to the leading figures of the Scottish philosophy of the period, David Hume and Adam Smith, that intellectual historians conventionally attribute the radicalization of the split, an attribution that has proved remarkably stable over the past half-century; and, indeed, there is some ground for it, for we have seen how Hume tried to shrink the term "reason" to facts and relations, driving a wedge between the "reasonable" judgments of fact and the passions on which action depends. Yet the development is more complex than the agreed story suggests. It turns on the ambiguous nature of the early-eighteenth-century project of turning Newtonian principles of observation and analysis back upon human behavior. "The proper study of mankind is man," as Pope had said.[5] Hume was heir to the hopes vested in this project; he thought that consistent correlations could be traced between reason and passion, sufficient to found a morality which, though functionalist, should be enough to elicit the reverence of thoughtful men. The clouds of Natural Law still scudded across the bright rationalist sky of the new "moral science." His twentieth-century interpreters have seized upon a famous paragraph in the *Treatise of Human Nature,* where Hume commented ironically on the failure of moral writers to explain the transition from "is" to "ought"; this they have understood as a direct avowal of the fact-value divide.[6] But it is far from clear that Hume's irony was in-

4. Something similar may be said about Bernard of Clairvaux's distinction of *contemplatio* and *consideratio.* See *De consideratione,* 1.78; 2.2.5.

5. Alexander Pope, *Essay on Man,* 2.2.

6. *Treatise,* 3.1.1.

23

tended to suggest that the transition was altogether impossible to explain, and more probable that he meant us to understand that he himself was the first to offer a successful explanation of it. And among the statements referred to as formed with the verb "is" he must surely have included some judgments of value which exceeded the limits of the "facts and relations" formula — e.g., "courage is a virtue." Almost all his own moral judgments are in fact formed in this way. The "is"-"ought" transition, then, is probably not from fact to value but from value to obligation. What concerned Hume at this point was what classical thinkers knew as the question of the good and the right.

The divorce of knowledge and will which became a preoccupation of twentieth-century moral philosophy marks a kind of philosophical boundary. Confronted head-on, it presents us with a *reductio ad absurdum* that must by some means be overcome. An argument between Philippa Foot and R. M. Hare which held the philosophical stage a generation ago was essentially about the terms and conditions on which philosophy could extricate itself from the expressivist dead-end into which it been backed absent-mindedly by Logical Positivism. Where Foot cut the Gordian knot by challenging the whole descriptive-prescriptive alternative and reasserting the value-bearing "is," Hare, though more respectful of the gulf, was no less resolved to bridge it, first by way of Kantian universalism and later by a variant of utilitarianism. Centuries earlier the high scholastics had sidestepped Abelard's voluntarism in a manner not unlike Foot's. There could be, they acknowledged, excusable ignorance of bare contingency, but there was also ignorance culpable in itself, simple inattention to the way things are, which, so far from excusing, actually incriminated us. Men and women usually sin with their eyes closed, and we recognize the rebellious will by the cognitive confusions that accompany it. We know what moral failure is by losing our way, in Dante's famous image, on our journey through the forest of the world.

So the protestation, "I am more to be lamented than blam'd, if I am mistaken" is, perhaps, more bravado than argument. We have limited sympathy for serious mistakes about reality. One who misses his father's funeral because he does not know of recent changes to the train timetable has all our sympathy; one who misses his father's funeral because he does not know that a father's death is a more significant event than a stranger's, has none. Those who persist in thinking that their friends are betraying them, that Jewish bankers are conspiring to undermine civilization, that Africans are constitutionally less intelligent than Europeans, etc., etc., are

24

not treated as good souls regrettably misinformed. We are much more likely to be indulgent to those of generally sound principles who succumb to moments of weakness. Even errors of circumstantial fact, about which it is easy for well-meaning people to be deceived, elicit a more complex reaction than mere sympathy. In 2002 it was widely, almost universally, believed by Western heads of governments on the basis of information supplied by their security services that the dictator of Iraq possessed, and was prepared to use, weapons of mass destruction. On the strength of this belief they went to war, but, dramatically, the information proved false. The difficult and risk-laden factual judgments political leaders make must indeed incline us to sympathy, and yet we do not excuse them of responsibility when they make them wrongly. And that is not only because politicians are, in a special sense, peculiarly answerable to those they represent. It belongs to the whole logic of practical reason that we need to know what we need to know. "Believe me, king of shadows, I mistook!" cries Puck.[7] Is that an excuse or a confession? It is both: in disavowing "wilful knaveries" that Oberon would charge him with, Puck must acknowledge "negligence." To excuse himself on one front, he accepts blame on another. "I mistook" is a confession, and if it is not the most self-abasing confession we have ever heard, perhaps it is the most common. Mistakes are not the high peaks of guilt, but neither do they lie on the plain of innocence. We differentiate "mere" mistakes from bad intentions, vices of character, and so on, in an ascending scale of moral seriousness, yet behind moral failure at every level lies a failure, temporary or permanent, circumstantial or structural, to keep our actions in tune with reality.[8]

The Poles of Reason

Ancient philosophy knew of a polarity which it described in various ways and sometimes found troubling; one common terminology spoke of "the pleasant" and "the honest," another of "ends of good and evil" (*fines bonorum et malorum*) and "obligations" (*officia*). "Good" and "evil" represented the order of value that we find in the objective world; "right" — and

---

7. William Shakespeare, *A Midsummer Night's Dream*, 3.2.
8. Among those who have stressed this point most effectively in recent years must be mentioned Pope John-Paul II. Not for nothing was his great encyclical on moral theory called *Veritatis Splendor* rather than *Voluntatis Rectitudo*!

its opposite, "wrong" — represented the obligation that determines the scope for action lying before us. But the dialectical relation between these two poles could, they feared, too easily fall apart. Cicero, who often reflected on the problem, explained how the good and the right could become disconnected, with disastrous results. "There are several schools of thought whose initial assumptions about the ends of good and evil effectively subvert their account of obligation. Posit a supreme good disconnected from virtue, conceive it in terms of assets rather than right, and stick to it consistently without reference to natural decency, and you will have no friendship, no justice, no generosity."[9] And again: "Once pronounce anything to be worth pursuing, once reckon anything as a good other than what is right, and you have extinguished the very light of virtue, which is simply what is right. You have overthrown virtue entirely. . . . Either this point must be firmly maintained that what is right is the sole good, or it is absolutely impossible to prove that virtue constitutes happiness, in which case I do not see why we should trouble to study philosophy."[10] Speaking here through the mouth of Cato the Elder as a representative of Stoic principles, Cicero assumes that "happiness" is the same as our experience of "the good," and on that basis makes three claims: (i) that there cannot be two distinct and unconnected sets of principles, one about what is good, the other about what is right; (ii) that a distinction between "the right" and "the good" can only be a conceptual one, since in all concrete judgments the two must coincide; and (iii) that the right, which he calls the "light" of virtue, is epistemologically decisive, while the good, the happiness which virtue "constitutes," has ontological finality. So, Cato argues, we learn what is good for us simply by consulting our duties, not *vice versa*. The right and the good are like Prime Minister and monarch: the right is devoted to serving the good, while exclusively dictating policy.

---

9. Cicero, De officiis, 1.2.5: "Sed sunt non nullae disciplinae, quae propositis bonorum et malorum finibus officium omne pervertant. Nam qui summum bonum sic instituit, ut nihil habeat cum virtute coniunctum, idque suis commodis, non honestate metitur, hic, si sibi ipse consentiat et non interdum naturae bonitate vincatur, neque amicitiam colere possit nec iustitiam nec liberalitatem."

10. De finibus, 3.3.10f.: "Quidquid enim praeter id quod honestum sit expetendum esse dixeris in bonisque numeraveris, et honestum ipsum quasi virtutis lumen exstinxeris et virtutem penitus everteris. . . . Nam nisi hoc obtineatur, id solum bonum esse quod honestum sit, nullo modo probari possit beatam vitam virtute effici; quod si ita sit, cur opera philosophiae sit danda, nescio." The term honestum is, perhaps, not quite as narrow as "right," conveying less suggestion that there is just one right thing to be done in any situation.

Why can we not have two distinct sets of moral principles? We may, it would seem, go through life comfortably enough, pursuing happiness where possible and doing our duty when it thrusts itself on us without ever resolving in our minds the relation between the two. We do some things because we want to, others because we ought to; these two practical reasonings are different, and we hope for a life in which a certain balance can be struck between them. This view has had some recent popularity. But it does not help us think about the *struggle* of duty and inclination, which is a major feature of moral experience. True, we may not experience this struggle much of the time, and we may form the impression that some people (though hardly the most admirable) never experience it; yet the very fact that we distinguish these terms as opposites shows our awareness that a struggle may arise. We would not say, "This is my duty," if we did not mean, "I am not doing this just because I want to!" And there are some whose life for one reason or another is a constant struggle, those who can never visit a restaurant without conscientious inquiries whether what is set on the table was organically grown, humanely reared, and fairly traded. These may look for more guidance from moralists than the banal observation that their duty lies with free-range organic farming, their happiness with the skills of the chef. Not to interest ourselves in how the right and the good relate is simply to live the unexamined life. Human beings may do it, but philosophers may not collude in it. They have a responsibility for the unification of the moral field, bringing some order to the different claims.

To achieve that order requires some slackening of the stiff Stoic insistence that our duty is always plain to us, and we lack only the motivation to do it, a view which interprets the struggle wholly as one of will, not of reason. Is it not sometimes the other way round, that our duty is obscure but we know with reasonable certainty what will make us happy? Many critics, ancient and modern, have been willing to repose great confidence in the evidential value of human desires. Some have reposed too much. For even if I could get a clear view of where my own happiness lay simply by consulting my desires, that would still leave the happiness of the rest of the world out of account. In fact, of course, desire is an inconclusive guide even in my own case, for it is too unstable and inconsistent. So there is no more reason to expect that the good will be self-evident than there is to expect that duty will be self-evident. Lack of self-evidence is the essential reason that morality cannot depend on intuition, but always involves thinking. Yet moral thinking cannot ignore desires any more than it can ignore the sense of duty. Neither the one nor the other may afford us self-evidence, and yet they each afford us indications.

If the thesis that the right is epistemologically decisive fails, what of the claim that the right and the good converge? John Milbank has recently pressed the view that this, too, must be abandoned. The right and the good, he thinks, represent alternative metaphysics between which we must simply make up our minds. If we do so on Christian theological grounds, we shall conclude that the good *overcomes* the right; God's gift in history requires us always to take an open and welcoming, not a closed and controlling attitude to the emergent future.[11] The difficulty with this, as with the more overt antinomianisms which it seeks to qualify, lies in its unwillingness to take the status of obligation seriously, which leaves ethical discussion an artificially narrow range of things to talk about. What alarmed Cicero's Cato about the idea of unreconciled principles was that it overthrew virtue, i.e., left unresolved the question whether at any point the right thing was to be done. "If they were consistent," Cicero again remarked, "these schools of thought would have nothing whatever to say about obligation."[12] But we do persistently have things to say about obligation — Milbank himself does.

Goodness is an aspect of what *is,* rightness is what *is to be done.* If we call something "good," we cannot simply conclude that it is "right" without qualification. Right for what purpose? For whom? When, and in what circumstances? Not all that is good demands to be realized at this very moment in time, or by some action of ours. Bach's music is preeminent, to be sure, but does that mean that I put down my writing, or whatever else I happen to be doing, to listen to his music now? And is it never to be Mendelssohn or Elgar, those admitted lesser luminaries of the musical firmament? Evidently, there is a time for not listening to Bach. Yet there must be *some* practical implications of thinking Bach's music preeminent. It must be right to encourage musicians to include Bach in their programs, and listeners to have Bach on their ipods. A Member of Parliament once tried to persuade the British House of Commons to ban Shakespeare in schools on the ground that he was too good a writer to allow the young to have him spoiled for them by the rigors of the classroom. This bizarre proposal had

11. John Milbank, "Can Morality be Christian?" in *The Word Made Strange* (Oxford: Blackwell, 1997), pp. 219-32.

12. Cicero, *De officiis,* 1.2.6: *"Hae disciplinae igitur si sibi consentaneae velint esse, de officio nihil queant dicere."*

the merit, at least, of raising the question of how general admiration for the playwright might, and might not, shape an education syllabus practically. The goodness of good things constitutes a reason why *certain* acts at *certain* times are right; the badness of bad things constitutes a reason why *certain* acts at *certain* times are wrong. But there is a journey of thought needed to focus the wide-spreading "is" of value upon the narrow "ought" of an obligation to perform a given deed at a given time. Practical reason correlates the actions we immediately project with the way things are; it is to think, as the Psalm puts it, "*upon* his commandments *to do* them" (Ps. 103:18).

It follows that practical reason cannot be intuitive reason; it cannot pocket its ball in one shot. It has to negotiate a way between the two poles of description and resolution, the one determinate and the other indeterminate, one in the sphere of the actual, the other in the sphere of the possible. "Memory looks back, intention forward; the one must be knit to the other," wrote Augustine.[13] A pattern of argument familiar from the Epistles of the New Testament asserts a truth about God and mankind and makes it the basis for a command or recommendation: "Since, then, you are risen with Christ, seek those things which are above" (Col. 3:1); "since, therefore, Christ suffered in the flesh, arm yourselves with the same purpose" (1 Peter 4:1); or even, "I appeal to you, therefore, brethren, by the mercies of God, to present your bodies as a living sacrifice" (Rom. 12:1), where "therefore" connects the whole doctrinal argument of the first eleven chapters of Romans to the sequence of practical exhortations that occupy the remainder of the book. The New Testament constantly announces truths that are to direct our practical deliberations, especially truths about the goodness and severity of God and the death and resurrection of Christ. It expects us to take these truths as the ground for practical demands, and to return to them when those demands need confirmation or clarification.

When we try to describe this movement of practical reason between its two poles, a misleading analogy suggests itself. Theoretical reason, too, is discursive. An argument proceeds deductively by inference from premises to conclusions, and having reached its conclusions, rests in them, having run its course. Its conclusions, if validly reached, are just as secure as its premises were. So conclusions to one argument may supply premises for

---

13. Augustine, *City of God*, 7.7: "*Necesse est a memoria respiciente prospiciens conectatur intentio.*"

another, and in this way theoretical reason extends its kingdom inference by inference. It is tempting to construe practical reason on the same model. If theoretical reason proceeds from the known to the unknown, why should not practical reason proceed from the determined to the undetermined? The scholastics, Saint Thomas among them, were attracted by the analogy. They suggested that each of the two types of reason had its own set of first principles, or axioms, from which conclusions were drawn. Their operations were thus parallel and independent.[14] The influence of this conception on Kant's formulation of practical reason can hardly be overstated.

Yet it is mistaken. Practical reason is not deductive, but inductive. The parallel between the progress from the known to the unknown and the progress from the determined to the undetermined is merely apparent. Practical reason is not an inference from premises to conclusions. It has no premises, no points from which an uncontroversial start may be made, and it has no conclusions, on which its trains of reason come to rest. No premises, because the knowledge of the world on which practical reason turns is always contested knowledge, not agreed. No conclusions, because practical reason terminates in action, not in belief. The descriptive accounts of reality that afford an *entrée* for action are not agreed starting-points. They are complex readings of the world, and as such arguable from the beginning. Moral reason has, of course, its commonplaces and formal rules — "the good is to be pursued, the evil avoided," etc. — which work just like the formal rules of logic in theoretical reason. But these are not the substantive readings of the world and its order on which our judgments of the good are based. Disputes about the world mark all of our moral thinking this side of the vision of God; such are the cognitive conditions of the age of Ethics. Nor are the resolutions reached by practical reason resolutions *in thought*. They are moments of action which punctuate thought without bringing it to a final cadence. At a certain point the thinker lifts his head from his hands, sighs, and says "Well, there is nothing else to be done!," then picks up a pen and signs a document — or whatever it is he has been thinking about doing. The more climactic and self-conscious moments of this kind we call "decisions," and philosophers have sometimes spoken of decision as an "eruption" into the midst of thought. We need not be so dramatic. Not every moment at which thought passes into action is a Rubicon crossed or a die cast. So we speak more generally of "resolutions,"

14. Thomas Aquinas, *Summa Theologiae*, 2-1.91.3.

a word that includes longer-term determinations, broad policies of action, the pursuit of general principles for living, some of which may never actually come to the point of being consciously decided on, but simply form in the mind. Yet whether climactic or incremental, resolution is action and not thought. It does not round off a train of practical thinking in the way that a logical conclusion does for a theoretical argument.

When Fermat's last theorem was finally proved, what was left for mathematics to do but contemplate the proof? The proof is everlasting; the question once disposed of is disposed of forever. But of no practical question is this true. When the document has been signed, we may still go on asking about the rights and wrongs of signing it. The deed itself is beyond correction, so that the question has ceased to be deliberative, and has become reflective. Yet in its new form it continues to be put: *should it have been* signed? That phrase "should have been" has not received half the attention it deserves from moral philosophers. We are hugely, and perhaps dangerously, comfortable discussing what should and should not have been. Of course we may pull ourselves together, and say, "There is no point in asking that anymore!" But to stop asking is *itself* a decision, for we are perfectly able to go on asking the question and may sometimes be unable to stop. And since other deliberative questions may turn on the answers we give to this reflective question — not least whether, and how, we should repent of what we have done — it retains a practical significance.

So practical reason is not deductive, which is to say, unidirectional, moving from a point established to a point still to be attained. It moves to and fro between the world of realities and the moment of action; it correlates a description of the one with a determination of the other. We have introduced two terms which refer conveniently to the two directions of practical thought, from description to resolution, and from resolution back to description. We have spoken of *deliberation* and *reflection* respectively. The metaphors contained in these two words suggest the contrast clearly: "reflection" is "turning back" on something that is already there, "behind us" as it were; "deliberation" is "weighing up," facing an alternative, looking at possible courses of action that have not yet been resolved. More simply, we may speak of "thinking about" and "thinking towards."

To clarify what should already be clear: the distinction between deliberation and reflection does not correspond to the distinction between practical and theoretical reason. Practical reason includes *both* these movements of thought, reflection as well as deliberation. Deliberation cannot stand on its own without reflection, nor can reflection stand on its

31

own without deliberation. On the one hand, any thinking-towards needs some thinking-about as a springboard from which to take off. One may act without thinking at all, but one cannot think-towards acting without thinking-about some truth of the world in which one will act. One cannot think-towards a policy of buying fair trade tea or coffee without thinking-about the problematic balance of power in the world's tea and coffee markets. The question "what am I to do?" means, "what am I to do *in this state of affairs?*" — and so always presumes an answer to the question "what state of affairs?" Practical reason, as we have said, has its own stake in descriptions of reality. If I ask whether pains in the left side of my chest are the first signs of a heart attack or merely an acute costochondritis, I have a strong practical interest in a truthful answer. Similarly, reflection points on towards deliberation. The proposition that God loves the world is in itself a work of reflection, a determination of the truth of things, not a decision to do something, yet we have not grasped its full significance unless our minds are led on to how we may conduct ourselves in a world that God loves. The same is true of propositions that have no reference to a transcendent reality, but deal with any important reality, with famine, art, politics, or whatever. Reflection in isolation becomes, as we say, "abstract" or "theoretical," and unless we are subject to the discipline of a discourse authorizing abstraction — a theoretical discourse such as theology, aesthetics, politics, etc. — we regard it as lacking semantic legitimacy, and call it "insincere," meaning that it is careless of the real significance of what it speaks about. What has happened when we think and speak insincerely is simply that we have *not* thought — or if we did think, we have stopped thinking too soon.

Responsibility

The traffic of thought we have described between the good and the right, the determined and the undetermined, is characteristic of all practical reason. Yet some practical reason is entirely trivial. When I find a Phillips-head screw of 2 mm. diameter buried in a piece of wood, and select the appropriate screwdriver from my kit to get it out, I am thinking practically. And that means I am thinking discursively, for even though the skilled handyman can dispose of the matter in a flash, those of small competence in such matters, as I am, know that there is a train of thought involved in identifying the right tool for the task. In everyday speech we distinguish "practical" thinking of this purely technical order from "moral" thinking. What is it that makes the difference? Merely to say that one is trivial, the other serious, begs the question: trivial and serious in relation to what? The difference is that moral reason has a third focus of attention: it must consider not only the world of reality and the moment of possibility, but the acting self. To the practical question of how the world (reduced, perhaps, to the shape of a screw) affords opportunities for action (in the shape of a screwdriver), moral thinking adds the question of how this action may determine the successful or unsuccessful living of a life.

Sometimes the answer is, Not much, and that is why not every practical question has a significant moral dimension. There are many things and qualities within the world which, good creatures of God as they may be, do not of themselves present a challenge to the human self and its living of life. There are "things indifferent." We can take them or leave them. I can praise the Creator for white-flowering hydrangeas while planting the blue varieties. Even indifferent things, of course, can assume a grave importance circumstantially. If someone calls out, "It is heavy!" as I stoop to lift a box of books, or "It is red!" as I career towards a traffic light, I treat these observations as warnings of serious responsibility. Yet what gives them that significance is not their content; heaviness in boxes and redness in lights are of themselves of no more significance than white and blue in hydrangeas. They borrow their momentary significance from the practical conditions in which we shelve books or drive cars. Moral qualities, on the other hand, are always and necessarily relevant to our agency. If someone asserts that an unspoiled valley is beautiful, a plan prudent, or an act treacherous, a claim is laid on me which is always and necessarily important. No human being can ignore it and live life successfully.

This third point of reference does not add a further stage to the discursive journey of thought in reflection and deliberation. It does not provide additional or more decisive reasons for doing something (like stopping at a red traffic light) which we already had reasons for doing, that our hope of heaven or fear of damnation may be involved. Rather, it gives a reason for treating the complex of action and reasons-for-action with heightened seriousness. The conduct of the matter assumes great importance; the whole world (from the point of view of own destiny) depends on it. We may perceive this immediately, in the sense that the fact affects us before we know how to express it. It may sensibly be called an "intuition," and around the immediacy of this moral perception there have arisen moral theories which we call "intuitionist" or "emotivist." We cannot find fault with them for seeing that this is a moment of simple awareness, a non-discursive perception of urgency and peril that weighs upon the agent's soul. Urgency is a fundamental aspect of moral reasoning. But these theories draw the wrong inference from it. They generalize the intuitive character of this moment of perception to the whole train of moral reasoning, attributing our resolutions to something like "an inbuilt homing device" (an unfortunately memorable phrase coined a generation ago by J. A. T. Robinson).

What needs to be clear is that moral thought is not just practical thought played *con brio*. Merely to talk about the practical project, the movement from reflection to deliberation, is not yet to talk of what makes this project a grave and important one, a "moral" undertaking. We must penetrate behind it, to give a thoughtful account of ourselves as those who entertain and pursue the project: what is this life about, which this action of mine contributes to? what authorizes me to be an agent in the first place, and what impels my action? Moral thinking is self-direction and needs, therefore, to get a purchase on the self, not only on the direction. The moment of heightened moral sensibility accompanies an act of perception which can be successful or unsuccessful in the same way as any act of rational perception, i.e., true or false. If the cognitive character of the moral perception is not recognized, the necessary questions do not get asked of it. Strong moral feeling cannot be a moral conclusion in and of itself. Intuitionist theories thus tend to make the perfectly ordinary phenomena of moral questioning unintelligible by drowning out the uncertainties with the *fortissimo* brass of strong moral feeling. As one critic has well said, intuitionism "wants to know too much about values, and to know it too quickly."[15] There may indeed be flashes of light, moments when we say — perhaps of a calamitous war or famine — "Something was radically wrong with the policies that got us to this point!" But these moments are the beginning, not the end, of a train of moral questioning.

We speak in this connection of *responsibility*. The confused appearance of this term in twentieth-century Ethics is due to its promotion in differently weighted senses in the German-speaking and English-speaking worlds. From Max Weber there derives a use locating responsibility specifically within the political sphere, where it stands for something like "realism." "Responsibility-ethics" (*Verantwortungsethik*) is contrasted with

---

15. Jean-Yves Lacoste, *Le Monde et l'Absence d'oeuvre* (Paris: Presses Universitaires de France, 2000), p. 123.

"intention-ethics" *(Gesinnungsethik),* and connotes a readiness to take full cognizance of the outcomes of any decision and a rejection of the principle that the ends cannot justify the means.[16] The Weberian responsible statesman is a Promethean figure, answering *to* himself alone *for* everything that happens. Never excusing his failures to achieve his ends by attributing them to adverse circumstance or hostile resistance, he answers for them in solitary grandeur — to himself. It is, one might say, the moral epitome of sovereignty-theory, and leads in one of two directions. Either it may tend to its formal opposite, unaccountability, since answering for oneself to oneself is so remote from other rational communications that it quickly vanishes into nothing at all. This is what has happened when a rogue statesman appears before the public to say, "I take full responsibility," conceiving that he has found a magic spell to make his critics go away. Alternatively, and more commonly, it may lead to madness, as with poor King George in Bennett's play, believing that "I make the weather by means of mental powers."[17]

From H. Richard Niebuhr there derives another use of responsibility, associated with the self-reflection of the active subject.[18] Niebuhr's work on this theme, cut short by death, bears every sign of its unfinished status: important explorations of moral subjectivity are tangled up with the author's fondness for "fundamental-motif analysis," so that "man the answerer" is pitted against "man the maker" and "man the legislator," each of these hominids supposedly contending for a different object of Ethics, "the good," "the right," and "the fitting." In fact, if one knows the proper use of the words "the good" and "the right," one knows why the addition of a third member to that pair is unthinkable and an "ethic of responsibility" surplus to requirements. But the *concept* of responsibility is not surplus to requirements. The term names not a program, not a system, but a moment

16. "Politik als Beruf" (1919); English translation, "The Profession and Vocation of Politics," in Max Weber, *Political Writings,* ed. P. Lassman and R. Speirs (Cambridge: Cambridge University Press, 1994), pp. 309-69. The interpreter of Weber is left with the problem of knowing whether the rejection of "intention ethics," identified, disturbingly, as the ethics of the Sermon on the Mount, is intended only in relation to political reasoning or, as parts of the argument suggest, is meant to be total. Hans Jonas made notorious use of Weberian "responsibility" in his radical proposal for an authoritarian political ethic to deal with a global emergency (*The Imperative of Responsibility: In Search of an Ethic for the Technological Age* (Chicago: University of Chicago Press, 1984).

17. Alan Bennett, *The Madness of George III* (London: Faber & Faber, 1992), p. 57.

18. H. Richard Niebuhr, *The Responsible Self* (New York: Harper & Row, 1963).

— just one moment, but an important moment — in such ordinary, commonplace moral thinking as every John Doe engages in. For all his confusion, Niebuhr understood why the idea was important. Responsibility is an awareness of ourselves as subjects of action, as those who conduct the passages of thought between world and time, who come to resolutions of which they know themselves to be the author and understand the weight and significance of what they do.

In much modern discussion the term stops a gap left by the shrinkage of the traditional Christian term "conscience." "Conscience" in Christian vocabulary once had a wide range of reference: not only to judgments we pass on our own deeds, but to the whole range of awareness a moral agent can command, to the "consciousness of" this or that, and indeed to the agent's own self, characterized morally as true or false, pure or compromised. In the modern era, however, it became reduced to a moment of feeling, painful or complacent. Talk of conscience thus left out the all-important question of the subject and significance of this feeling: whose consciousness was it, and what did it tell him about himself? Left as a point without dimensions, it was bound to be pulled in opposite directions by the poles of practical reason, towards saving the appearance of the world at one moment, towards seizing the occasion of action at another. So conscience was split in two: the "reflexive conscience" accusing and excusing on the basis of objective reality, and the "prospective conscience" pushing forward to greet its moment of opportunity. Assuming this pathologically bipolar character, now inflated with the opportunity for self-creation, now deflated by the objectivity of the historical self with its inexorable limitations, conscience became a god, commanding the world to exist anew, and at the same time a demon, subjecting the self to impotence and causing it to wallow in self-contempt. Conscience was certainty — the German word *Gewissen* is closely connected with *Gewissheit* — while at the same time conscience was doubt, doubt to the point of panic about loss of competence for action. Without a substantial center, the responsible self oscillated in the pendulum-swing of practical reason, re-living the fate of Icarus in Greek myth, rising to the sun on self-made wings and falling to destruction. Thus the modern conscience posed a dilemma for agency, and became a dilemma itself.

An important experiment in moral theory, which enjoyed some prominence in recent decades, hoped to recover a substantial place for the agent-self by way of a different kind of discursive thought, narrative. This experiment began from dissatisfaction with a case-oriented approach which seemed to reduce the subject-matter of moral reason to practical problems. Moral thinking was more than mere problem-solving, it said with perfect justice, because it asked and answered the questions of agent-identity: Who am I that act? By what right do I come by the responsibility I recognize in myself? Agent-identity was then explored in terms of narrative, giving an account of the subject's origin and destiny that would "situate" the subject as a formed quantity within the world and history. But this solution recreated the dilemma of conscience in a new form. Looked at from one point of view a narrative identity is no more than an inert fact, an outcome of historical forces that do nothing to clarify responsibility. A thousand examples of social-scientific "explanations" illustrate the point: born in poverty, brought up without love, set loose upon the world without education, how can my story be an account of responsible freedom? It is simply a reason to believe I have no such thing! Looked at from the opposite point of view a narrative identity is *already* an assertion of my freedom, which assumes the garb of history as a convenient disguise. Born in poverty, brought up without love, set loose upon the world without education, I boast of my power to disturb the settled order and impose my will; but how can such boasting constitute an account of responsible freedom? It is merely a justification for the ways I have used freedom, or failed to use it. Narrativism has not been sufficiently on guard against the temptation to self-justifying bad faith: many an "I" has been glad to borrow a specious dignity from some story or other to clothe its carryings-on. Neither has it been on guard against the temptation to despair of responsibility, to wear one's story as it were a mourning garment for one's life, as a way of avoiding living. Either the narrative situates the self in world and history, stripping it of responsibility, or asserting responsibility it makes free with a constructed world and history. In telling my "story" I *project* my agency onto the screen of historical facticity, a projection that falls one side or the other of the point of freedom which I exercise. What is needed is not the narrative self-as-object, framed against the background of real or imagined history, but the responsible self-as-agent, emerging out of history precisely for the task that lies before it.

Narrative ethics was right to seek a ground for the self's historical substance, but sought it in the wrong place. Competence for freedom is not a gift that history can give; it must be received from a source behind history. Unless we know our history not merely as a narrative of origin but as a divine call, we cannot grasp our freedom, for freedom is nothing else than that same call renewed, with pressing effect, in the present. And this is the point of truth behind the constant but difficult-to-formulate intuition that morality cannot be sustained without religion. *Some* level of morality can be, of course, but not the full sense of responsibility which makes us feel that morality matters. God's call to us to serve him is the content of our responsibility; it is the security our competence may command in face of the imprisoning facticity of the past and the dizzying indeterminacy of the future. Centered and secured by this call, we are not swallowed up by what has been, not dissipated in what is yet to be, but can exercise our freedom in identity with ourselves.

Ethics and Prayer

And so, as we press back to what moral thinking presupposes, we come face to face with the relation of the self to God. There is no moral thought that is not, quite simply, human thought, no human being that was not born to think responsibly about being, living, and doing; yet there is no moral thought that does not depend for whatever effect it may have upon a gift for which no human source can be credited. The relation of the self to God may or may not be consciously recognized, but whether it is or not, it underlies the sense of responsibility which gives the moral its character of urgency. But to the extent that it becomes conscious, it becomes explicit. Developed and self-conscious moral thinking begins and ends by calling on God.

"Invoking God" was named by Karl Barth as "the basic act of the Christian ethos."[19] He seized rightly on the fact that the teaching of the Lord's Prayer comes at the center of the Sermon on the Mount. But we would fail to get to the root of Barth's intentions if we left the phrase "Christian ethos" standing on its own, and thought of prayer as a kind of spiritual sublimation, effected by revealed religion, of a rational and worldly "natural ethics" that knows nothing of prayer. Prayer is such a human act that even those who acknowledge no positive belief in God or in prayer itself may catch themselves performing it. Derrida cannot be denied his prayers and tears.[20] Prayer is the form thought takes when we under-

---

19. Karl Barth, *The Christian Life: Church Dogmatics,* IV/4: *Lecture Fragments,* trans. G. W. Bromiley (Grand Rapids, Eerdmans, 1981), p. 102.

20. Cf. John Caputo, *The Prayers and Tears of Jacques Derrida* (Bloomington: Indiana University Press, 1997).

stand that agency implies a relation to the government of the universe, at once cooperative and dependent. It is precisely as prayer that moral responsibility may be assumed: "Watch and pray, that you enter not into temptation!" (Mark 14:38) In prayer we declare our practical destination as human beings before the power that can bring our calling to effect. If, as Barth says, the vocative, "Father!" is "the primal form of thinking, the primal sound of speaking, the primal act of obedience demanded of Christians," we must specify that this vocative is demanded of Christians simply because it is offered to humans.[21] Yet prayer, like moral thinking, can be malformed, and malformed in the same ways. The rightly formed petition is at the same time the rightly formed train of moral thought.

Here lies the double importance of Jesus' teaching of the Lord's Prayer. The "we" which calls upon the Father in Heaven for daily bread and forgiveness of sins is mankind made articulate and ready for active life before God. The prayer itself has a tightly conceived formal structure. After its first address to the Father in heaven it attends to God as (in Jüngel's fine phrase) "the secret of the world," and to the world as the scene of God's self-disclosure: "on earth as it is in heaven." That phrase qualifies not only "Thy will be done," but the two preceding petitions, too: "Hallowed be thy name," of which Luther liked to say that it asks for God's name to be hallowed "among us," and "Thy kingdom come," which looks for the fruition of the purposes for which the world is designed.[22] At this point in the prayer the agent's self and time enter the picture, in want of the conditions, material and spiritual, for action. "Give us this day our daily bread" attends to the day of our own exertion, which is also, therefore, the day of our need. The petition for forgiveness looks for liberation from the constraints of the self's past, a liberation which must be open to all, if it is open to any. Finally, standing on the threshold of agency and conscious of the peril of loss, the agent looks to God for a future that will affirm and not destroy the point of human action: "And lead us not into temptation, but deliver us from evil."

Three points of commentary with which the synoptic evangelists surround the teaching of the prayer reinforce its importance as a training in

---

21. For this interpretation of Barth's intentions, cf. Eberhard Jüngel, "Invocation of God as the Ethical Ground of Christian Action," in *Theological Essays*, ed. and trans. J. B. Webster (Edinburgh: T&T Clark, 1989), pp. 154-72.

22. ". . . that the name of God, which is altogether holy in heaven, would also be precious and holy among us" (*Sermons on the Catechism 1528*, trans. John W. Doberstein, *Luther's Works*, vol. 51 [Philadelphia: Fortress, 1959]).

the active life, an ordering of practical thought. In Saint Luke's Gospel (11:1-13) Jesus picks out for commentary the opening words, the invocation of God as Father, in one of the most characteristic of his many teachings about petition. We evil men know how to give good things to our children, even to our next-door neighbors, when they ask; so we should ask, seek, knock. Those resonant three verbs impress upon us the urgent application required. No time here for the speculative doubts of a theosophical age about the effect of petition on an all-knowing God, no time for the scrupulous doubts of a universalist age about petition for one's private needs. Those who hear that threefold command are bent on the active tasks of life, urgent for the conditions of success.

Saint Matthew, however (who also knows and elsewhere uses that teaching on petitionary prayer) frames the Lord's Prayer in a different way, with warnings against exaggerated public piety (6:1-18).[23] The Lord's Prayer is a corrective to the all-too-extensive repertoire of petition that pagan spirituality deployed before its gods. Prayer can ramble diffusively, can spin itself out, can take a wide view of the world and all its fascinations. Prayer can be a spectator sport, something like reading the newspaper, clucking solemnly or chuckling merrily at the tragicomic display of the human scene. It can sweep its eye grandly over the multitudinous classes of mankind and their needs, pause intrigued over the details of some minor endeavor, pretend to all the powers of omniscience in scanning the horizon and zooming in on the intimate scene. It can forget that those who pray are men, not God. The churches of Jesus Christ, heedless of his strictures, afford multitudinous examples of imitation pagan prayer each Sunday, having learned to discard (even in self-styled "liturgical" churches) the virtues of a well-designed petitionary form in favor of the luxuriant ramblings of extempore, a trend which goes well with the fashion for resting complacently on the buttocks rather than pressing forward upon the knees. What is lacking in this broad and benevolent oversight of the world in all its largeness and its smallness is the urgent *intentional focus* that belongs to the partnership of man with God. Diffuseness is a great dissipater of attention. If God calls us into partnership, and makes himself partner of our endeavors in prayer, we had better come to the point, and quickly.

But this is not the only contextual feature that deserves notice in Saint

23. For a fuller treatment of the context in the Gospel of Matthew, see my "Prayer and Morality in the Sermon on the Mount," *Studies in Christian Ethics* 22/1 (2009): 21-33.

Matthew's presentation of the Prayer. Jesus picks out for commentary the petition "Forgive us our sins, as we forgive . . . ," and this affords us the third and most important perspective on our practical and moral thinking.

On the face of it the condition of mutual forgiveness is a simple requirement of distributive justice with its customary disdain for favoritism: we ask nothing for ourselves that we are not prepared to give to others. But that is to miss the most important thing about the petition, namely, that it is for *forgiveness,* and forgiveness is for the unjust. We would have no business asking distributive justice of God, nor promising it, for when it comes to justice one cannot pick and choose; the act of judgment, if it is to take shape in history at all, must take shape in all its forms, retributive as well as distributive. Otherwise there could be no continuity of judgment; it would have to start afresh from moment to moment, a stalling sequence of new creations in which the justice of one moment would be cancelled out by the justice of the next. But new creation is precisely what this prayer is about — if, that is, we know what we ask when we ask for forgiveness, and seek something more radical and more real than an indulgent adjustment of the scales in our favor. We ask for discontinuity, for the inauguration of a new justice. To desire pardon is not to desire that God should wink or bend; it is to desire that he should show himself in his majesty as the one who raises lost mankind from the dead. It is to ask something that of its nature transforms the world, and with the world our neighbor, our enemy, our established right and identity. We had better not ask for that new moment of possibility if we do not want it, if we are not committed to acting on the answer as it is given. But if we ask it, we had better be ready for it on its own terms, peopled as it is by all who stood in need of forgiveness, our own forgiveness as well as God's, and now stand in need no longer.

What has this prayer for new creation, we may wonder, to do with the logic of moral agency? Action depends for its intelligibility upon a strong continuity with the past, a context given from past to the present, since the future we face is contentless and undetermined. All we think we know about present and future is by borrowed light from the past. The prospect of new creation, then, would seem to be the defeat of agency, a prospect in which we cannot be in identity with ourselves, knowing who we are, where we stand or what is to be done. But there is also a newness that belongs essentially to agency. To project action is to conceive an initiative which, however it must be understood in categories mediated by our past, is not determined by the past. Action asserts freedom against sheer facticity — here, at least, the Arminians of the seventeenth and eighteenth centuries understood rightly. That we should be more than creatures of our past, more than mere continuers of it, that is the gift presupposed in our creation; it is the power which nature's creator bestowed on creation's lord.

And when we are effective lords of creation no longer? When our self-determination has been used to destroy our freedom, and what should be intelligible has become unintelligible, what should be new is old, even before it is brought to pass? Then we can only ask God for the greater miracle of a new newness and a new oldness — a new possibility of initiative which restores and renews the relation to the past as well as the future. That is what is articulated in the prayer, "Forgive us our trespasses, as we forgive." Not that even in the days of our original freedom we could take the gift of newness and intelligibility for granted as an immanent power just like the natural power to move our limbs. Action was always a venture upon the course of events, always dependent upon the cooperation of divine Providence. "Prosper thou the work of our hands! O prosper thou our handiwork!" (Ps. 90:17) we might imagine as the morning prayer of Adam and Eve in Eden. But now, born slaves, we stand in need not of God's cooperation, simply, in bringing new out of old, but of a "renewal" of agency, of "the washing of regeneration and renewal in the Holy Spirit" as it is described (Titus 3:5). The supreme power of the act of God the Redeemer lies in those repeated "re-" prefixes, the power to make again without unmaking, to make that possible which has previously been made impossible.

For a final word of interpretation we turn back to the concluding observation of Jesus on the Lord's Prayer in Saint Luke: "If, being evil, you know how to give good gifts to your children, how much more will the heavenly Father give the Holy Spirit to those who ask him?" (11:13) It is for the Holy Spirit that we ask when we ask to receive and grant forgiveness, and in every other petition of this prayer. It is for the Holy Spirit that we ask whenever we think what we are to do in full consciousness of the conditions of our agency. At the heart of moral thinking is a prayer for the coming of God to reshape our freedom from within: "Come and recreate mee, now growne ruinous."[24]

---

24. John Donne, "A Litanie," in *Divine Poems*, ed. Helen Gardner (Oxford: Clarendon, 1952, 2001), p. 16.

CHAPTER 3

Moral Communication

The "I" and the "We"

The moment of responsibility, charged as it is with self-consciousness, presents an opportunity for self-deception. A brief passage in the Epistle to the Galatians directs our attention to it: "Bear one another's burdens, and so fulfill the law of Christ. For if any one thinks he is something, when he is nothing, he deceives himself. But let each one test his own work, and then his reason to boast will be in himself alone and not in his neighbor. For each man will have to bear his own load" (6:2-5). The self-deception consists in supposing that he, the individual member of the body, is "something" when he is "nothing." He is nothing, that is, if he stands apart as a positive "something" on his own, detached from the mutual exchange of burdens. It is an easy misunderstanding to fall into when he considers his own agency, the "work" through which he has actualized himself. But that work, Paul remarks, requires "testing," and by what standard can it be tested other than by its context in the life and work of other people? When it has passed *that* test, when its bona fides as an expression of mutual support is established, then indeed it can be a ground for individual confidence, or "boasting." A secure sense of "I," no longer as nothing but as something, arises precisely from its place within the "we."

There is something paradoxical in this. It seems to fly in the face of a certain self-evidence about the "I" as the subject of practical and moral reasoning. When I conceive and plan my actions, I have a sense of being alone. That is not a mere illusion; an initiative lies with me, and I am answerable for it. When in the Psalm the wicked declare, "Our lips are our

43

own; who is our master?" (Ps. 12:4), they are perfectly correct as far as they go; nobody initiates their speech for them, nobody takes responsibility for it from them. Yet the content of their planning and of the speech that passes across their lips is far from original to them. Conceptuality, grammar, vocabulary, and syntax are all on loan from the community which supports them, and which they serve, in this case, badly. Even their desires have a strong cultural component. They have their moment of initiative, but it is an interim moment. Behind and before their private devisings is a very public discourse about the good, a discourse on which they depend and to which they will make a difference, whether as contributors or predators. The agent-self is not a Newtonian atom prior to all combinations; it lives on its imports. None of us is a competent agent if we have not become aware of the social underpinning to our individual agency. That is part of what it means to be a *person,* a subject of action constituted not by a nature but by a place within a community of persons.[1]

"Many there be that say, Who will show us any good?" For the poet of the fourth Psalm, that question was a shrug of cynicism and despair. The many who said it assumed that the answer was, Nobody. There was no good to be had or to be done, none, at least, within their reach. But the poet does not agree. He answers their question, obliquely, with a prayer: "Lift up the light of your face upon us, O Lord!" Hans Ulrich has argued that the importance of the question and the answer lies in the question's form, which turns the pursuit of Ethics in a new direction, away from the indeterminate object of study, "the good," to the possibility of a determinate disclosure of the good: *Who will show* us?[2] In that Ethics searches for a concrete good, a good that arises before us here and now within the possibilities of life and history, it is not like solving a mathematical problem, in which either you reach the answer by a disciplined process of thought on your own, or you don't reach it at all. Here there is something to be pointed to, identified; there is the possibility of being *shown.* But that focuses the question, "Who?" The first and last pointer to the concrete good is divine providence. But in between the first and the last there is another, intermediate pointer: other people may show us the concrete good. Moral thinking is of its nature a *communicative* inquiry with a social basis.

Philosophy, which has often wrestled with what it calls "the problem

---

1. On this I have learned much from Robert Spaemann's *Persons: The Difference between "Someone" and "Something"* (Oxford: Oxford University Press, 2006).

2. Hans Ulrich, *Wie Geschöpfe Leben* (Münster: LitVerlag, 2005), p. 86.

of other minds," came only late in the day to suspect that there might be a problem with *this* mind. However, a modest thesis of the social construction of the self is, perhaps, generally accepted now in a philosophical milieu that has listened to Wittgenstein. Even the mid-twentieth-century existentialists, who appeared to speak on a more strident individualistic note, recognized the force of the prior social context. In stressing the need for individual agential "authenticity," in urging us to "become an individual," they recognized that individual agency can never be taken as self-evident. Thinking one's own thoughts and deliberating one's own course of action is, after all, something to be learned, an acquirement to be won; the condition of winning it is to know with some clarity how, and on what terms, one's action belongs to its social context.

This modest version of the thesis is enough to explain the all-important role of *discussion* as a matrix for our moral thinking. Discussion is so important, indeed, that we engage in it for pleasure as well as at need, and constantly pursue it in imagination as well as in actual society. And yet our models of social interaction usually misrepresent it, conceiving of it as a kind of negotiation or bargaining. In striking a bargain we start out with an idea of what we want to achieve and negotiate away as little as we can. In a discussion we start out with less than that, and end with more. Beginning from an intuition, we use the dialectical interplay of perspectives on a shared question to help us "know what we think" and "make up our minds." A negotiation succeeds when it achieves a compromise; a discussion succeeds only when it reaches a measure of substantial agreement. Discussion is a shared struggle to reach truth and overcome error. It may often unfold in an eristic form, as an exchange of arguments and rebuttals. (We see this especially in the phenomenon of the combative personality, the individual who has difficulty thinking through anything at all without picking a quarrel, thrusting discussion-partners into the role of opponents.) The eristic form has its own right. Differences at the outset provide the stimulus for thought to progress dialectically. As we know from politics, discussion cannot get off the ground if either party denies the other the right to its independent starting point; when the condition for entering discussion is that a key point is surrendered in advance, no discussion can occur. Paradoxically, then, discussion depends at once on conflicting assertions and on mutual concessions. But what is asserted and what is conceded are not the same. We may enter a discussion in perfect confidence that we are in the right against our opponent. We may be sure that once we have explained ourselves fully, no shred of an answer can be made. Yet we may still sense the need to prove our impregnability in a clash of steel, to gain real knowledge of what the opponent actually says when confronted with our case and to discern, if we can, what alternative resoning can be brought to bear against our own. Even the most confident discussant can expect to learn something from the exercise.

Let us suppose that I disapprove strongly of the death penalty, and take up the cudgels against someone who defends it. As our discussion proceeds, certain things will become clear. One is that there are various reasons for disapproving of the death penalty, some of which may plausibly claim a perennial moral truth, while others are more circumstantial. If my opponent forces me to think hard, I shall understand better what social and historical conditions have made the death penalty appear reasonable to past generations, and I shall have to ask whether those conditions could ever recur. I shall come to see that my view of the matter is part and parcel of a wider philosophy of penal justice and governmental responsibility, and I shall be forced to elucidate that philosophy more fully and to test its capacity to shed illumination on other questions, too. None of this could I have gained from talking to those who agreed with me. What it amounts to is that if at the end of the argument I still say, "I disapprove of the death penalty!" I know much better than before what I mean by it.

All of which is accounted for within a limited version of the social-construction thesis, that discourse is a necessary matrix for mature individual moral thought to emerge. But we should not be content with so limited a version. Individual moral thinking is social not only in its beginnings but in its ends. Our most secret deliberations, our most independent conclusions, are directed towards a community of understanding. We think as though trying to win the approval of a judicious audience hidden in the darkness of the stalls, ready to applaud our point of view when the lights go up. It is not simply that without a community of inquiry our thought cannot begin. If we cannot envisage a community of agreement, our thought cannot have any end in view, either.[3]

When parties to a discussion punctuate it with decisive stands expressed in the first-person singular ("I passionately oppose . . . !") that is neither the beginning nor the end of moral thought. It is a moment in-

---

3. Here we may profit from the insight of the social behaviorists of the first half of the last century. Cf. George H. Mead, *Mind, Self and Society* (Chicago: University of Chicago Press, 1934), p. 141: "One inevitably seeks an audience, has to pour himself out to somebody. In reflective intelligence one thinks to act, and to act solely so that this action remains a part of a social process."

between, a moment at which the common inquiry has broken down and the common agreement at which thought is aimed has disappeared from view. The affirmation of the "I"-position is a strategy for regrouping and relaunching the discussion, as when a standard is thrust into the ground and the scattered soldiers gather to it. Rhetorical inebriation may make the standard-bearer forget that he is part of an army, but that is the logic of it. In the moment of affirmation the "I" takes responsibility for the whole, making a decision on what must be held in common by all. And so together with the right of a distinctive point of approach must be granted also an anticipation of persuasion. Serious discussion is entered expectantly, with a view to finding a common perspective which makes sense of differences and does justice to what is important. At the outset this is *only* an object of hope, still to be looked for; yet it is something to be discovered, not devised. It is not a negotiated add-on to the prior private convictions of the discussants; it is the realization of those convictions, which, though they may have been held privately, were intended socially.

For the content of our separate convictions is already universal in intention. To think in moral terms, however out of step with one's fellows, is to think about what is fitting to the human race and about the fulfillment of human existence. It is to think *as* a representative human being, one whose relation to the world and other humans must be determined not for oneself alone, but for all. This is what we say when we claim, "It is a matter of principle." What is to be determined in this case is universally determined; it is to be held as a truth for the world. That is why we may feel ennobled by our quarrels and disagreements, our dignity and honor enhanced by the sense that we do not take a stand for ourselves alone.

We can throw this aspect of the thesis into sharper relief by a political illustration. There is a financial crisis, and the question of the day is what the Chancellor of the Exchequer ought to do. Different voices are raised to give different answers: the editorials and comment columns of the media are full of it, the Members of Parliament press home their rival answers in media interviews, the university has seminars with papers and responses by qualified pundits, party headquarters prepare scoping-documents to lay out politically acceptable alternatives, while in the Treasury itself officials labor over it with memoranda and minutes. At the breakfast tables of the nation the same question is chewed over every morning with the toast. Nobody finds it strange, apparently, that everyone is debating what *someone else* is to decide and do. Yet we ought to find it strange. What is going on, apparently, is a kind of third-person deliberation, but deliberation is thinking-towards-acting, and so, it would seem, inescapably first-person. There is, of course, a wrong explanation that lies seductively to hand: only the Chancellor himself actually deliberates on the principal question, what he himself is to do, and everybody else deliberates on one of an infinite number of different subsidiary questions, the Treasury officials on what advice to proffer, the parliamentarians on how to position themselves in the political arena, the press on which constituency of the readership to curry favor with, the breakfast tables of the nation on how to vote at the next election, and so on. To each, we may be tempted to say, his own agendum — except for the university seminar, which, as a theoretical inquiry, does not engage in deliberation at all, but studies the Chancellor's deliberations from the infinite height of scholarship as it might study the historical deliberations of Winston Churchill. This explanation has, of course, a limited bureaucratic truth in describing the distribution of immediate practical responsibilities, but in trying to persuade us that we have all been discussing different things when we imagined we were all discussing the same thing, it is flying in the face of common sense. We are right to think we have been discussing the same thing. Behind the question of what the Chancellor is to do there lurks the question of what *we*, as a political community, are to do. That is what the question of the Chancellor's best course of action really means, and that is why we can, and must, all deliberate on it together. The Chancellor will act representatively for the nation, and so the nation deliberates with the Chancellor, each of us deliberating representatively for the nation. Representation is not simply a matter of the elected status of a minister within a democracy. Democracy itself is founded on the more fundamental political reality that there are such things as peoples which think through representative citizens and act through representative officials. It would be the same if it were the Governor of the Bank of England or the Queen. Without the *collective* subject of action there is no democracy, no Chancellor, no Chairman of the Bank, no Queen, no citizens, nothing, indeed, to be decided and no one to decide it.

Moving beyond the political context something quite similar may be observed. The simplest individual activities acquire their meaning from common social undertakings. Consider such a day-to-day matter as slowing down to a stop at an intersection with a major road. It is I who got into the car of my own accord, and drove off; so it is I, and nobody else, who must put my foot on the brake. Yet to give an account of what I am doing (to my child, say, who is urging me to take the crossing at seventy), I must point to a set of communicative assumptions and expectations which I had no hand in shaping but which frame the intelligibility of my actions. Without them I could not form the idea of a "major" road, nor assign a significance to a thick white line painted across the highway. My practical thinking continually alludes to ends pursued in common by the society I belong to. They enter my personal self-directive deliberations when I think with my own head and dispose the movements of my own limbs. The common undertaking does not detract from my individual sense of agency, and may even positively enhance it as I take upon myself the dignity of a communicated expectation. Dutifully stopping at a red light in the dead of night, with empty roads stretching in all directions and no sign of another vehicle, I may feel some complacency in my little demonstration of competent social performance.

Advice

The term "collective" is, of course, a tendentious one, and may be taken to imply the obliteration of individual initiative. Our interest lies with a "communicative" action, which elicits and supports individual agency, sets it appropriate goals and assists its mature exercise. If our communications sometimes aim at binding collective resolutions in which the individual is caught up willy-nilly, they may equally often aim at opening up free space. Here we shall reflect on forms of communication where this is especially true, *giving advice, obeying authority,* and *moral teaching.* All of these are indispensable to our exercise of freedom.

One who gives advice draws alongside another person and shares his or her deliberations. It means thinking, as it were, on two fronts at the same time, not only asking, "What are *you* to do?," but also, "What am *I* to say about what you are to do?" When two friends disagree about something in the news — let us say, some controversial biotechnical innovation — they may argue the matter hotly and toughly, each seeking to persuade the other by every strategy of reason that looks likely to overcome resistance. They do not ask themselves what they *may* say to each other, only what there *is* to say. But suppose one of them is actually employed in biotechnical research, and has serious conscientious anxieties about the work the laboratory does. Then the discussion takes on a different character. The two are no longer (to borrow Habermas's phrase) in "discursive equilibrium"; the friend is under strong constraints as to what may be said.

What has made the difference is the moral danger to which the princi-

pal agent is exposed: danger, on the one hand, of sacrificing moral integ-
rity to a career; danger, on the other hand, of sacrificing prospects for self
and family to a whimsical scruple. Advice is the assistance offered to an
agent in danger, and that is why there is disequilibrium built into it. It
comes to the aid of one overwhelmed by a challenge to moral discernment.
Advice may be of help to someone faced by that challenge by bringing to
bear an independent view of it. Though subject to restraint in the way it is
offered, that independent view is essential: without it there could be no
counsel, nothing to shore up the tottering agency of the principal. The
condition of saying anything helpful by way of advice is that the two differently placed discussants can find a point of convergence where their outlooks meet. Yet an adviser is entitled, may even be obliged, to hold back
from expressing convictions he or she may hold, in order to keep space
open for the principal.

In the face of someone's moral danger the adviser is asked for an exercise of imagination, in which she hypothetically projects herself into the
place of the other and brings the two perspectives together. Talking to
someone contemplating suicide, I must ask myself the hypothetical question about my own possible suicide, a question which in my ordinary life
experience does not arise very much. Could *any* circumstance justify me in
taking my own life? Though the first-person question assumes a hypothetical form (not, "What am I to do?" but, "What *would* I be bound to do, *if*
my case was as yours is?") the answer is not an empty speculation. I must
give it with commitment and accept responsibility for it. "If it were my
own child," says the doctor, "I would agree to the operation." That gambit
wins the parents' confidence, and rightly so, because the doctor, occupying
for a moment the place of a father or mother experiencing the terrors of a
child's illness, is committed to the point of view he has adopted hypothetically. It is almost a kind of promise to feel the outcome as the parents will
feel it.

It is important to see what work this hypothetical version of the first-
person singular question is *not* doing. It is not judging by the criterion of
what I myself actually feel, or want. On the contrary, I am being required
to take the measure of *your* feelings and wants, to see the practical question
from an angle not my own. But neither is it simply repeating back to you
the feelings and the wants of which you have told me; an adviser is not an
echo chamber. I have to place myself in *your* position, with all its awareness
of peril; but I have to place *myself* there, together with the convictions,
principles, and — for the time being, at least — comparative self-

possession that I would bring to any other task. In making that conjunction of outlooks I draw on stocks of knowledge and experience I have already acquired. My advice will be as good as the wisdom I can bring to it; advising is an art, not a technique. Which does not mean that the adviser comes ready with an answer. Imagining the other's position, the adviser deliberates afresh: what are the circumstances and constraints? what general moral principles apply? It is an exercise of intellectual application which should leave one wiser. But a well-formed knowledge of good and evil has to underpin this imaginative adventure. Like all arts, advice has its objective basis. Otherwise principal and adviser would simply collude with each other, the principal seeking not advice but endorsement, the adviser taking the cheapest route to gratitude and appreciation.

This imaginative conjunction of outlooks is what we call "sympathy." Sympathy is quite different from actually having, or having had, similar experiences. I may never have despaired to the point of wanting to kill myself; I may have no experience of an unplanned pregnancy; but in sympathy I can conceive the despair and enter into the panic. Experiences of a closely similar kind can in fact be a doubtful asset, for they risk drowning out the other's experience with their own too-sharp memories. Battered wives are not always best advised by battered wives nor bullied children by other bullied children. Those who have been closely involved in similar situations may fall into bad vicariousness: instead of taking on the experience of the other, they may ruminate on their own, using the other as a screen to project what they have undergone themselves. An adviser must offer a point of objectivity: the adviser's "I" and the principal's "you," starting from their different situations, seek to converge upon the common "we." Its basis is a moral wisdom that belongs to us as a human community, universally. Suicide, abortion, standing up to violent husbands, cheating in business, and bullying of children are all "our" questions before they are your questions or mine. It is because the questions are ours, as members of the human community, that one of us can dare to offer advice to another about them.

The role of the adviser is to bring the sufferer out of isolation back into contact with the original community of human moral discourse. And this accounts for the restraints upon the adviser's role, which are needed in order to safeguard the space for the principal's own agency. For the moral danger does not consist simply in the possibility of making the wrong choice, but in the possibility of failing to reach a clear and authentic decision for which he or she can take responsibility. Anyone who has often given advice knows those times when the obvious recommendation sits on the tip of the tongue, but must be held back until the principal comes to find it for him or herself.

There is a second reason for restraint. Advice has a particular situation in view, and there are aspects of the situation which only the principal agent can know. It may make a great difference in a damaged matrimonial relationship whether and to what extent the estranged couple still, despite everything, love each other. Only they can say. A third party may show them why it is important to be clear about it, but not what the truth of the matter is. Even this, however, does not reduce the adviser to a mere sounding board. For every difficult and painful situation there is a repertoire of stock descriptions, clichés, proverbial wisdoms, on which people will draw in good or bad faith to interpret to themselves and others what they experience. And because, as the saying goes, you can itch without knowing where to scratch, such clichés suck troubled spirits into their current. Many a couple declares, "Our marriage has been a hollow sham for years," when they have only recently been conscious of a difficulty. The wise adviser can spot the cliché, and help them test it for its substance.

These two considerations are weighty reasons for restraint in giving advice, yet it is possible to exaggerate their weight. An adviser may be *too* overwhelmed by a sense of the impressionability of the principal, *too* anxious not to abuse the advisory position, can forget that the common search for understanding requires a certain willingness to expose the common moral questions. Failing to credit the principal with a mind of her own, the adviser can make a fetish of saying nothing. But an adviser who gives no advice, gives no help. Non-directivity and "authoritarianism" (which is, of course, different from authority) are cut from the same cloth, both of them over-conscious of the adviser's power over the principal. The abuse of power may, in fact come from the other side. The principal, too, may be able, and tempted, to control the adviser, and this results in a curious form of mutual abuse: demanding and offering advice in which the adviser does not believe.

Not every request for advice, not every attempt to give it, can be successful. The meeting of perspectives may fail to happen; the adviser may not be able to offer advice, or the principal to accept it. In giving and receiving advice we are not always capable of honesty, especially when we feel ourselves injured and wanting support. These hazards heighten the importance of personal trust in the relationship, and so make the professionalization and bureaucratization of advice-giving especially problematic.

Authority

When one who faces moral danger seeks advice, it is not just any advice that is looked for. There is, of course, the phenomenon of the one who rushes round seeking advice from everybody; but we usually look on this as a kind of incompetence. The competent agent looks for the right person to seek advice from. And the right person is not necessarily the best friend, the most admired teacher, or the most powerful connection. It is whoever is most likely to command a comprehensive understanding of the situation, and so to be able to suggest a clear and convincing path of action. It is *authoritative* advice that is looked for. But what is authority, and how does it come about that one person has it and another does not?

Authority I take to be an *event in which a reality is communicated to practical reason by a social communication.* Unlike a purely theoretical disclosure, authority gives practical direction. Unlike a disclosure reached by independent insight, authority is mediated. It depends on the communicative event, as another's personal presence, activity or word, written or spoken, affords the agent a new perception of reality that is needed for effective action.

The reader who has not followed my previous wrestlings with this theme over some decades is gladly excused a brief stock-taking at this point. In *Resurrection and Moral Order* I proposed that authority was "the objective correlate of freedom," a thesis to which I have continually returned. It seemed to me at the time, as it seems still, to be a fundamental principle for understanding the matter. Put in more classical terms, it means that freedom and obedience correspond, an idea familiar to Ambrose and Augustine, the germ of which can be found in Romans 6:18. Freedom depends on obeying, and in obeying freedom becomes possible. All this must be said, and yet freedom is a *wider category* than authority, so that my phrase was too loose to make a satisfactory definition. Not every exercise of freedom is, directly at least, a response to authority. Authority is not simply vested in the world, self, and time as soon as we awake to them. That would collapse the dialectic of freedom and authority onto a flat plane, reducing all authority to self-evidence, all obedience to commonsense. The word "authority" would then refer to no more than that worldly reality which so hugely interests us anyway, the word "obedience" to no more than the purchase offered for our self-fulfillment by the firm surface of reality. And that is why my account of "moral authority" in *Resurrection and Moral Order* was flat and this-worldly. In studying *political* authority subsequently, especially in *The Ways of Judgment*, I laid more emphasis on authority's lack of perspicuity, and this emphasis must now be accommodated within the general theory. I am prompted in part by a re-reading of P. T. Forsyth's *The Principle of Authority* (1913), in which the miraculous and providential aspect of its operation is always kept to the fore.[4] Authority, we must say, is a *focused disclosure* of reality, one that demands we turn our attention away from everything else and concentrate it in this one place.

Authority has a bottleneck form; the perception of a reality demanding action is filtered through a focused disclosure. Reality is shown us, but instead of seeing it whole, entire, and in the round, we see it through this demonstration, this personality, this theory, this command. All that may be said or thought about the matter in hand is implied; were it not so, I should not find the disclosure authoritative. Yet if all that could be said or thought were immediately evident, I should not need the disclosure at all. Without disclosure there is no authority; there is only unaided understanding on the one side, brute exercise of power on the other. The confused elderly patient being bundled off to hospital, who cannot understand why her familiars insist on it, the complacent sage who (as in Kant's much-quoted remark) approves the teachings of "the Holy One of the Gospel" because they are what he always thought anyway, are neither of them capable of receiving a disclosure, neither of them capable of responding to authority. "There are good reasons for this, which I dimly perceive but do not fully comprehend!" — that is the characteristic form of recognition we accord to any authoritative utterance. That is the best reason available to us in the circumstances. Faith in things unseen is always an element in practical reasonableness. The communicative framework of our practical reasoning does not allow us to take in the complete picture straight off.

Authority penetrates social existence and gives it cohesion. Discomfort with authority in general (as opposed to discomfort with this or that exercise of it) is discomfort with society itself. Liberal and egalitarian philosophy is perfectly clear-sighted in distrusting authority, for authority undermines the presumption that society is a contractual relation among equally self-possessed adults, a presumption which screens out, in Martha Nussbaum's apt phrase, "all the times of asymmetrical or unusual dependency . . . through which all citizens pass."[5] Authority is the correlate of

---

4. P. T. Forsyth, *The Principle of Authority in Relation to Certainty, Sanctity and Society* (London: Independent Press, 1913, repr. 1952).

5. Martha Nussbaum, *Hiding from Humanity: Disgust, Shame, and the Law* (Princeton: Princeton University Press, 2004), p. 311. I owe this reference to Joshua Hordern.

freedom: within our social communications the moment of initiative is given to us. But each moment of initiative is preceded and prepared for, since none of us enters the world with a private store of wisdom, goals, and purposes, but only with those that have been lent us by others.

Authority is implied, then, in a very broad range of social phenomena: in teaching, learning, questioning, associating, admiring, and loving, quite as much as in governing and obeying. So broad a range, indeed, that the two ideal types, the authority of the teacher and the authority of the ruler, may seem not to capture all the instances. There is, for example, an authority of practical effectiveness; "nothing succeeds like success," the proverb tells us, and an evident achievement of any kind attracts a following. And there is an authority of beauty; those who look great and make us laugh or cry when we see them on the screen can win respect for their opinions on politics or the best detergent. Where would modern democracy be without both of these?

To give more nuance, then, to the traditional alternative of intellectual and political authority, we may identify two spectra on which instances of authority may be ranged. There is, on the one hand, a spectrum of *practical immediacy*. Although authority always has a bearing on what we do, a disclosure may shape our exercise of freedom more proximately or more remotely. Intellectual authority is practical — but at one remove, shaping the ideas which will form the basis of our action. An "authoritative" scientific theory or theological doctrine may have no immediate implications for how I spend my money, but it will at least shape my worldview, which will have a ripple effect upon my practical assumptions. An average group of humanists with little first-hand basis for judging the merits of rival theories in Physics is more likely to chat politely in general academic company to a Nobel laureate than to a discredited rival. A politician with little interest in the Trinity is more likely to pay a courtesy call on the Pope than on the head of the Church of Scientology. Such is the authority of established theory. At the other end of the spectrum my physician's (still purely intellectual) authority may persuade me to undergo some very unpleasant treatment, though the understanding he conveys to me, cast in laymen's terms, is as remote from my powers of judgment as the theories of a Nobel laureate. The difference lies simply in the immediate practical relevance of the physician's theories to my needs.

There is, on the other hand, a spectrum of *cognitive plenitude*. Nothing can be thought or undertaken to any effect unless some truth about the world undergirds it. But since all the truth of the world is not digested in one gulp, and getting to know the truth and our place within it is a slow and complex matter, the relevant truth must reach us through a series of experiences, memories, reports, any one of which can be set aside and qualified by any other. We do not have the luxury of perfecting our knowledge before we set our foot upon the path of action. Truth is mediated in successive moments, giving direction step by step when and as we need it. So while every authority presents *reasons* to act thus and not otherwise, it presents these reasons without their being wholly conspicuous. They are implicit, only partially disclosed; we must act according to a truth we have only imperfectly grasped. Yet one exercise of authority may disclose a more extensive view than another, and it is this that makes the difference. Those whose power of speech — explaining, clarifying, making the mysterious plain — commands our believing adherence exercise "intellectual authority," the authority of wisdom. The teacher who first opens a disciple's eyes gestures towards a wide horizon.

Communication is the key. Knowledge uncommunicated, however great, is socially unfruitful. (There is, it must be confessed, a slightly desperate air about the great libraries of the Western world, so full of books unread from century to century; but at least the books are there, and encourage us to hope that we may, one day, get round to reading more of them. More desperate by far are the unread bibliographies of our scholarly writings and the databases of our online bookstores, where so much intellectual labor is reduced to a miniscule electronic note!) Intellectual authority is connected with speech used to good effect, the ability to deploy language powerfully and clearly. "The tongue of the wise commends knowledge, but the mouths of fools pour out folly" (Prov. 15:2). The relentless output of gabble never compensates for loss of articulate control. Acquired skill in the resources of language, its vocabulary, linguistic structures, and rhetorical organization, is essential to framing and focusing the nuanced discernment of reality. It sustains authority, and when it falls into decay, authority falls with it. Linguistic impoverishment in a community causes the most urgent expressions of concern to be dismissed as subjective opinion, and drives the structures of its government away from subtle discernment back upon the crude manipulations of power. Such is our age, which congratulates itself that language evolves, while forgetting that it devolves. Such are our great enterprises with their large budgets and tiny dictionaries, and such is our public discourse, where a leader's incapacity to construct the simplest sentence is seen as a strong political selling point.

The authority of wisdom marks one end of the spectrum of cognitive plenitude. At the other end stands political authority. In making certain practical determinations on behalf of its subjects by the simple exercise of its power to make them, it secures their acceptance on no other basis than the bare fact that they are made. When we conform to some bureaucratic regulation — let us say, by purchasing a vehicle license to keep a car on the public road, paying so much for it and no less, paying it to this body and no other, by that date and no later, the claim of the regulation on our understanding begins and ends with the fact that political authority has made it. Why the tax is so much and not more or less, why the date for payment is when it is and not earlier or later, why this body and not some other is charged with collecting payment, is immaterial. Knowing the thinking behind the details adds nothing to its authority. Yet, even so, there is something we can and must understand in general terms. Arrangements of this kind are needed if we are to enjoy the security of driving on safe roads, and official bodies are needed to promulgate and enforce them. A perspicuous understanding of the state's role in serving the common good contributes essentially to the authority of its regulations. Prescriptions carry no authority in themselves, however insistently made. Which is not to say that there are no occasions on which someone may simply issue a command — "Get dressed at once and come down to the station to answer some questions!" — but unless there is a context to make that demand intelligible, it is not an exercise of authority, but of power. Acts of power may be authorized — and even contribute to authority — but they are not in themselves acts of authority. Acts of authority need intelligible contexts. There must be a ground for them, even if it is only *raison d'état,* which is still a ground that can be understood and interrogated. Political authority is more than the simple exercise of power. Though it needs power to sustain itself, it also needs a minimal degree of common understanding. Yet *only* a minimal degree, for promulgation is nine tenths of the law.

"All authority is from God," we are told (Rom. 13:1); yet all authority is, at the same time, of the world. It is an attribute of social communications. The divine in its sheer absoluteness has no "authority," only control. The hidden God operates behind my back, unseen and unknown; he elicits my anxiety and fear, not my freedom and love. But the divine has not remained apart in hiddenness, but has shaped a world to ground our being, a covenanted sphere of communication between himself and ourselves, evoking agency and practical reason among us. Divine authority begins with God's self-disclosure in creation and providence. The Book of Job knows that the angry skeptic can recognize divine authority only when God "answers" (38:1). God's authority is God's entry into communication, his assumption of the direction of human life. That takes the form of prescription and command, though it takes many other forms, too. Yet the commands have authority because they, too, mediate God's presence to the world as creator and sustainer. Not their mysterious interruption of our lives, but the promise of fulfillment they bear with them, makes them authoritative.

Yet though all authority is communicative, not all communication is authoritative. When we say that authority is "of God," we point to the mystery that some communications have it, and not others. This, for Forsyth, was an essential clue. "Who shall explain the secret of the influence of one person on another? Authority is in the nature of a miracle, as appears every time a man quells a mob."[6] By containing such authoritative moments the world shows itself porous to God's miraculous activity. Here, taking his model from a political miracle, Forsyth concentrates upon the minimal end of the spectrum of cognitive plenitude, failing, I would think, to give sufficient weight to the purpose and moral order of the world *as creation.* Authority is worldly, and the world does not exist without a form or meaning, waiting for God to approach and bear down upon my soul with his holiness. Perhaps that is why Forsyth's concept of the ethical never really broadens out beyond a pinpoint moment of motivation, never takes in the breadth and scope of wisdom as it is spoken of in the Old Testament. With this qualification, however, we can embrace the thought that authority is God's "approach." Christians have spoken of world-order not only as created but as *sustained* by the constant activity of God, and the event of "authoritative" disclosure belongs to that sustaining work.

Apart from divine purpose for the world there could be no disclosure of meaning within the world, and so no authority of any kind. When our imaginations drain the world of final causes, its forms crumble into mere facticity before our eyes. Like everything else worldly, institutions which appear authoritative at one moment can appear arbitrary the next, as soon as we ask ourselves why they should be thus and not otherwise. Authority in worldly institutions rises and falls, as in those ancient kingdoms where each monarch reigned a year before being slain by his successor. (The elec-

6. Forsyth, *Principle of Authority,* p. 58. This miracle he calls "holiness," by which he means an attribute of God himself, but seen through the presence of God in the world, especially in ethical motivation and the justified conscience of the believer. Authority is God's "approaching," when "all the holiness of God bears down upon my soul," pp. 28, 40. Authority, Forsyth tells us elsewhere, is "the central question of religion, and therefore of everything," p. 17. That *order* of stating the matter is, I believe, absolutely right, though Forsyth gives too short a shrift to "everything."

tion cycle of modern democracies curiously reinvents this ritual, ensuring that a government that can do no wrong when first elected mutates predictably into one that can do no right!) Worldly authority asserts itself, and is discredited, discredited as soon as it occurs to us that it asserts itself *only to be* discredited. Yet even then we are not done with authority. That very moment of sad wisdom which disillusions us, as it seems, with all pretensions of authority whatever, is itself a moment of authority. What is this pathos of emancipation from imprisoning perspectives but the pathos of a new wisdom, commanding us in order to liberate us? Authority is an event which continually and repeatedly occurs, wave after wave of disclosure breaking over us, knocking us down and carrying us along, winning our recognition by the sheer certainty with which each new successive event presents itself. Institutions are formed around authority-events and renewed by them, but institutions are secondary. The event itself overwhelms and refashions the institutions. The Scriptures speak of "authorities" ranged alongside "angels," "principalities," "powers," "dominions," "thrones," and "rulers of this world," structuring forces that determine patterns of social existence, yet doomed to be overwhelmed because all forms of authority must in the end be taken up into the original, but powerful for the moment in that they mediate the original to us. God answers Job not out of the temple but "out of the whirlwind."

We have an intuition of this when we speak, using a common phrase, of "moral authority." What can be meant by this, given that all authority is *prima facie* moral anyway? It is as though we were searching for an authority that is more authoritative than authoritative, that is *really and truly* authoritative — as in the Irish joke about the *double* yellow line at the edge of the street which tells you not merely that you mustn't park there, but that you mustn't park there "at all, at all." It expresses our uncomfortable sense that authority contains antinomies. The rift between the two ideal types of authority, intellectual and political, is itself unsettling; neither, it would seem, can be wholly authoritative without the other, and yet we have no apparent ground to suppose them complementary. We are made anxious by political authority's reliance on the bare fact of its assertion; we are made anxious by scientific authority's reliance on bare facticity of the world. The voice of nature mediated through our fellow humans demands that we exist socially, yet our freedom insists that this voice produce credentials higher than nature. Apparently we cannot be at home with our fellows or our freedom until the dialectic of nature and history is brought to a resolution by some word that commands them both.

Moral Teaching

Moral teaching is a communication specially occupied with this word. In it the "we" of moral discourse has opened up into an "I" and a "you," a teacher and a disciple, a relation of authoritative communication. But not every authoritative communication is moral teaching, only that in which the authority behind authority is the *object* of communication, and in which the *goal* is the liberation of the disciple to understand and live well. Teaching is an act of witness to the authority which authorizes it, yet at the same time an act of nurture. It is comprehensive in its scope, coherent in its content, instructive and liberating in its effect. It does not consist of isolated observations or insights, but is "a teaching," a doctrine that can put us in a position to live our lives in harmony with nature and events.

Historically this was what was meant by "wisdom." There are many words of insight, many moments of intellectual achievement, always jostling and competing among themselves. The elementary literary form for communicating wisdom is the collection: proverbs about this and about that, proverbs confirming or contradicting other proverbs. The wise men of Israel, among others, were esteemed for collecting them and also for ordering them, as we see in the editorial note accompanying the book of Qoheleth (Ecclesiastes), which speaks of "the Teacher's" gift of "weighing, studying, and arranging" proverbs (12:9), and adds, with a telling simile, a justification for the single-author book, an innovation in Wisdom literature: wise sayings are "like goads," but the collected sayings of one man are like "nails driven firmly home" (12:11). Goads make animals jump, but nails hold things firmly in place. Eclectic human wisdom may be a stimulus, but it is inconclusive; it leaves the student as bewildered as it found him. What is needed is the doctrine of a single teacher, comprehensive, coherent instruction that does not stop at isolated observations but pulls everything together, liberating us to learn from them all and live in harmony with nature and events. Such a doctrine can dispose of the fragments of wisdom because it is authorized by the coherence of the world and its history.

We take the emergence of the great moral teachers for granted as a fact of history, as though it were an obvious and necessary development of the "axial era." But it was a remarkable phenomenon, this development of schools of disciples and traditions of teaching around the doctrine of a single teacher, often continuing many generations after his death. Philosophically, we tend to view the teacher as an irrelevance, allowing no middle term between moral thinking, on the one hand, and scientific ethical

reflection on the other. In the ancient world Plato doubted whether morality could be taught, while Kant spoke for the modern world in dissolving
the authority of "the Holy One of the Gospels" into the private approval of
his doctrines.[7] This reserve about teaching is not altogether unfounded.
What the teacher of moral wisdom hopes to communicate is at least cog-
nate with the student's disposition, if not already present in it. The chroni-
cler of history may impart a knowledge that the student simply lacked; but
those who receive and profit from moral wisdom are not altogether without it, as is shown by the fact that they receive it. Yet while nature, knowing
only generic truths and not disclosures, is as incapable of distinguishing a
successful moral teacher from a failed one as it is of distinguishing an en-
lightening proverb from an unenlightening one, history can tell of teachings which were not merely truths but discoveries, communications that
changed the course of events, which were not *of* the world, but came *to* it.
It can tell of schools of moral teaching that arose as hermeneutic traditions, receiving and exploring new discoveries in a variety of contexts and
defending them before a variety of challenges. It is against this background
that we may appreciate the force of Stanley Hauerwas's much-quoted
boast that "I tell my students that my first object is to help them think just
like me."[8]

In teaching, too, "all authority is of God." That such a figure as the
moral teacher should have arisen is a work of divine providence, recognized
by historical judgment. And that is why, whether expressly or by implication, a moral teacher is a religious teacher, one who has something to tell
about the doings of God in disclosing the way that it is open for men and
women to live. Ancient moral philosophy knew of the "demon" of Socrates.
And we may press this point further: whether expressly or by implication,
the moral teacher is a teacher of *monotheistic* religion. If a multitude of gods
figures in moral teaching, it does so as a harmonious chorus, not as a dis-
cordant contest of voices. Only so is the possibility given of *a* way that is
open for men and women to live. Socrates could be a moral teacher while
speaking of "the gods"; neither Homer nor Euripides could, for they
thought that to satisfy one god was to make an enemy out of another.

7. Immanuel Kant, *Grundlegung zur Metaphysik der Sitten* 4:408: "Even the Holy One of
the Gospel must first be compared with our ideal of moral perfection before he is cognized
as such." Trans. Mary Gregor, *Practical Philosophy*, Cambridge Edition of the Works of Immanuel Kant (Cambridge: Cambridge University Press, 1996), p. 63.

8. Stanley Hauerwas, "How We Lay Bricks and Make Disciples," in *After Christendom?*
(Nashville: Abingdon, 1991), p. 98.

As these scattered moments of enlightenment supersede one another and interpret one another, divine authority shapes the course of history as a whole, effecting a disclosure of the wisdom of God as a whole in which each moment has its proper place. Elijah, it was believed, must return and restore all things — morally, that is, by a doctrine that would put deep enmities to rest. And when John appeared in the wilderness and was taken for the Messiah, it was repentance that he was teaching. The earliest Christian thinkers never hesitated to think of Socrates and Paul as moments in a history of disclosure which reached its climax in the incarnation of the Word of God. At the center of that history Jesus of Nazareth, emerging from within a lively tradition of moral teaching that had grown up around rabbinic commentary on the divine law, was just such a great moral teacher as Qoheleth had envisaged. We say *more* than that when we call him Son of God, but we do not say something different, let alone contrary. The climactic disclosure of God's wisdom, giving history its final shape, was nothing less than God's disclosure of himself and the wisdom of his ways within worldly history.

> Thou'st light in dark and shut'st in little room
> Immensity cloistered in thy dear womb.

So John Donne, addressing the Virgin Mary, describes the Incarnation.[9] The "immensity" is not the immensity of the divine as such, but the immensity of divine wisdom *for the world*, the immensity of the *Word of God*. And the "cloistering" which Immensity undergoes in entering history has the characteristic bottle-neck form of authority: an infinity of reasons mediated through one comprehensive reason focused in the unique person, cloistered in Mary's womb, who represents them all. This authoritative word engages us for all authoritative words: for the authority of worldly reality in its many aspects, the authority of near relations and loved ones, the authority of civil society, the authority of our environment and its needs etc., etc. It is the evangelical mediation of reality, breaking into and re-constituting all our pre-existing traditions of wisdom about the world.

The teaching of morality is not a homogeneous intellectual enterprise. Within the complex variety of the world and its history there are many dif-

---

9. John Donne, "La Corona," in *The Divine Poems*, ed. Helen Gardner (Oxford: Clarendon Press, 1952, 2001).

ferent foci around which moral teaching can revolve: around community, around self-realization, around historical destiny, and so on. And between the observations of wisdom and the requirements of law, the one proposing insights into the world and the other proposing prescriptive directions of how social relations are to be conducted, there are many different forms in which moral instruction can be offered. Socrates, Confucius, Jesus ben Sirach, and Zeno all represent different interpretations of the task. Let us look, however, at the climactic instance, taking as our paradigm text the Sermon on the Mount. Its program of internalizing and radicalizing the Mosaic law follows the route of Jewish thought and sets this text apart from the more skeptical and conceptual questions of the Hellenistic world. The continuity of Jesus with Jewish traditions of teaching, suggested by Saint Luke's story of Jesus' childhood visit to the temple, was constantly emphasized by Saint Matthew. Yet by framing Jesus' Sermon as the teaching of a new Moses on a new Mount Sinai, and by including some of the strong claims he made for his own doctrine, Matthew points to a new departure, a breakthrough in the tradition, such as would later prompt Saul of Tarsus to find there the key to the obedience that had eluded him in the Pharisaic schools.

We may observe initially what this exercise of moral teaching does *not* attempt to do — and in this it is typical of all moral teaching. It does not attempt to give precise and concrete advice. Advice is occasional, addressed to the specific practical need of a given agent at a given moment. Moral teaching is different. It trains the disciple to think truthfully about what may need to be done. It is addressed to those "who have ears to hear," which is to say, those who will use their intelligence in framing their lives and making their decisions. It has enough generality to be valid from one situation to the next, transmissible from one disciple to another. Its purpose is to produce competent moral agents. And this is no less true of the Sermon on the Mount, where the context for all lives and all tasks is the newly pressing eschatological horizon. The text begins with a series of blessings that illustrate the climactic reversals that are to change the face of history; it continues with examples of the radicalization of the law in the dawning new age; it teaches about the purpose and context of religious exercises; it explores the pointlessness of anxiety; it displays through a wide variety of applications the law of equal returns; and finally it reflects on alternative outcomes of human lives that respond to moral teaching in different ways. Within this framework we can notice a number of different foci. Its descriptive content depicts God's attitudes to our practical engagements: "Your Father knows what you need before you ask him" and "If you do not forgive men their trespasses, neither will your Father forgive you your trespasses" (Matt. 6:8, 15). It describes the moral dispositions that will prove effective in the crisis of the world's transformation: "Blessed are the meek, for they shall inherit the earth" (5:5). Its prescriptive content contains broad moral policies, "Do not lay up for yourselves treasures on earth," and typical approaches to situations of moral challenge: "If any one strikes you on the right cheek, turn to him the other also" (6:19; 5:39). These typical approaches, highly pointed for pedagogical effect, fell victim to a literalist misunderstanding which gave rise to the unhelpful Protestant tradition of seeing the Sermon as "impossible" moral teaching that simply drove us back on God's mercy — an interpretation often thought of as Lutheran, though Luther's forceful commentary on the Sermon has more interesting things to say. This misunderstanding failed to comprehend moral teaching as a genre of communication, misconstruing as immediate instructions what were intended as typical approaches, to be thought about and given application as they prove applicable.

The Sermon also, and importantly, includes instruction on the hermeneutics of the prevailing moral tradition: "You have heard that it was said. . . . But I say to you . . ." (5:21ff.) For this is the "new law," distinguished from the old precisely by its readiness to go beyond simple prohibition and public regulation and to open up the meaning of obedience from the heart. That is the true sense in which it is "radical." More than any other ancient moral teaching it draws the disciple out from beneath the protection of accepted social norms and places him before God in full and truly founded responsibility.

At the very center of this text of moral teaching (6:1-18) there is the teaching of a prayer — not only *how* to pray, that is, but *what* to pray. Precise words are prescribed. If we have understood the relation of prayer to moral thought, we shall not be surprised at this. That such words should be open to private and public elaboration (*economical* elaboration, if we take Jesus' warning seriously!), that they should generate noble liturgies and passionate private intercessions may be taken as a matter of course. Yet the words are not merely an outline, a set of heads of advice or agenda items. They are themselves a possession of irreplaceable importance in forming the "we," the community of moral practice. That is why they should be placed — the bare text without embroidery or expansion — at the core of every Christian liturgy.

The conception of worship as magnified personal self-expression, a large-screen projection of the "I," obstructs the formation of the community by depriving lay members of the congregation of their proper ownership of the words of prayer. If the primary material for common reflection, replacing hymns and prayers that can be learned, possessed, and used by every worshipper, comes to be the spontaneous feelings of the minister and the autobiographies of selected model Christians, there is no room for the interaction of community and individual to develop. The model "I" overwhelms the (genuinely) personal contribution of the worshipper with a fake personality, imposing sentiments, moods, narratives, and reactions that purport to be personal but belong, in fact, to no actual person — not even to the minister, who affects them at the price of forcing his or her real personality into a straitjacket, trying to be the one single and embracing personality that will serve for all.

In traditional liturgies the occasional appearance of the first-person singular (in baptism and at the recitation of the creed) points to the Holy Spirit's grafting of the believer into the community. Yet its comparatively restricted liturgical presence and its total absence from the prayer Jesus taught, where the first-person is always plural, points to the common identity built up by prescribed prayer, the "we" within which each and every "I" can realize itself. The formal and predictable character of liturgy, giving us a purchase on the common "we," enables us to accomplish a personal self-offering *together with* all others who are gathered for worship. The liturgical constitution of the "we" is one aspect of what should be meant by that pregnant, if elusive phrase, "ecclesial density."

CHAPTER 4

Moral Theory

Ethics between Science and Practice

"Ethics" — let us use the term to cover the whole range of intellectual attention that is given to moral thinking and moral teaching by philosophy and theology. (Theories of morality emerging from the social sciences, and more recently the natural sciences, do not quite belong within Ethics for reasons that will become clear.) Ethics presents itself apparently as a discipline of study within the realm of organized knowledge. It claims to interpret, test, prove, and order the variety of things commonly thought and said in the ordinary courses of practical reasoning and instruction. "Moral Theology," which will serve as the default term for what is sometimes called Christian Ethics and sometimes Theological Ethics, assumes this interpretation and ordering into the hermeneutic framework of Christian Theology. Whether philosophy or theology takes the lead, we have to do with a modern theoretical endeavor, a rationally structured account of moral thinking and teaching which can be accommodated within the wider range of human knowledge as pursued by the recognized disciplines of study.

It makes little sense to distinguish Ethics from its parent disciplines prior to the emergence of Moral Theology in the sixteenth century. In theology the stream of godly knowledge flowed down uninterrupted from *sacra doctrina* to Christian life. The major moral texts of the patristic era were conceived as works of pastoral ministry, as with the writings of Augustine that shaped the Western understanding of marriage, or as works of ascetic instruction, as with the reflections on moral psychology from the authors of the *Philokalia*. To these genres the medieval theologians added the "disputation," which they hoped might be kept as short as possible.[1] The word "Ethics" appears in twelfth-century scholasticism to signal an engagement with the philosophical legacy of the classical past.[2] Yet the standard context for discussing conscience, virtue, and responsibility in the medieval period remained the theological *Summa,* while the *locus* for primary education on duties was a homiletic exposition of the Decalogue. The effect of the sixteenth century, however, was to separate what had hitherto been held together. A Protestant suspicion of the medieval entanglement of theology with law combined with a Renaissance aspiration to define autonomous disciplines of law and politics with their own (non-theological but not non-Christian) axiomatic starting points. On the Catholic side, the pastoral reforms of the Council of Trent required a discipline of pastoral training which absorbed the frontier of theology and law within the cure of souls.

The history of the modern ethical disciplines is still elusive, and we lack a comprehensive account. The development of Protestant Ethics, in particular, is hardly studied and little understood. Its differentiation from the Catholic current does not date back to the Reformation, but occurs around 1700, as part of that complex package of intellectual developments which, for convenience, we label "Enlightenment." Until the middle of the seventeenth century Protestant — and especially Reformed — moralists adopted patterns suggested by the Tridentine model and aimed at achieving a consistent and disciplined pastoral practice.[3] The solvents that caused the established forms of moral instruction to melt included, no doubt, a slackening of the will for church discipline in national churches persuaded of the need to tolerate dissent. Two other factors may be of equal significance. One was the emergence of a literary market for lay moral reflection in essay form or verse, a market catered for in England by writers such as Steele, Addison, Prior, and Pope. The other was the development, first in Germany and France, later in England and Scotland, of a

---

1. Cf. Thomas of Chobham, *Summa de Commendatione Virtutum* (ed. F. Morenzoni, CCCM 82B, pp. 87, 93): *"Officium theologi in tribus consistit, in lectione, in disputatione, in predicatione. . . . Et sunt fere eadem consideranda circa lectionem et disputationem et predicationem, scilicet brevitas et utilitas et liquiditas que excludit uanam subtilitatem."*

2. On the emergence and significance of the term *ethica,* the Introduction to *Peter Abelard's Ethics,* ed. D. E. Luscombe (Oxford: Clarendon, 1971), is instructive.

3. The father of Reformed Ethics, William Ames, was unusual only in his frank acknowledgment of Roman Catholic sources in his *De conscientia, ejus jure et casibus* (1630).

new style of systematic Philosophical Ethics for use in lay education. Such a work as Schottelius's *Ethica* (1669) was intended initially for grammar schools, but before very long Moral Science chairs appeared in the universities, and it was in this context that the pioneering Scottish school of Moral Philosophy arose, avowing, even while it understood itself as a Christian enterprise, Newton's mathematics as its intellectual model.[4] The eighteenth century, which saw the high point of Tridentine Moral Theology in such a figure as Alfonso Liguori, was, in the Protestant world, supremely the century of Moral Philosophy, culminating in the work of Immanuel Kant. But it was also the century of devotional revivals, which pressed home the religious significance of moral duties with urgency but little theoretical grounding. Two Anglican texts, published just two years apart in the same remarkable decade that saw Hutcheson's *Inquiry,* Swift's *Gulliver's Travels,* and the greatest work of J. S. Bach, illustrate how Protestant moral reflection had separated out into two contrasting but equally untheological streams: Joseph Butler's *Sermons on Human Nature* (1726) and William Law's *Serious Call to the Devout and Holy Life* (1728). The recovery of Ethics as a theological task was the work of the romantic reaction, attempting to overcome and to develop Kant's legacy. The credit for giving it currency must rest with Friedrich Schleiermacher, whose outlines for parallel Philosophical and Theological Ethics, though never advancing beyond sketches and lecture notes, were highly authoritative for subsequent generations. In the English-speaking world the recovery was comparatively slow to catch on, though it made faster strides in the anti-Erastian climate of the United States than it did in Britain.

The preeminence of the Newtonian model of science resulted in an uneasy cohabitation of Ethics with the sciences. The questions of moral reason — "What are we to do?" "How are we to live?" — are jokers in the pack of scientific play. Ethics is not distinguished from other disciplines by an "object" or "subject-matter" which defines its territory over against those of other studies of other objects. What kind of a thing is this morality, of which Ethics undertakes to speak? Clearly not a thing among other things, a segmented object of inquiry standing in relation to other objects as the locus of a certain body of evidence. Ancient Greek History may point to its archeological monuments, its epigraphical inscriptions, its

---

4. See George Turnbull, *The Principles of Moral and Christian Philosophy* (1740), 1.1. Introduction; Francis Hutcheson, *An Inquiry into the Original of our Ideas of Beauty and Virtue* (1725), 1.3.5.

historiographical texts, which distinguish it from, while making it compable to, Medieval Islamic History. For Ethics there is no such determinate body of evidence; everything is grist for its mill. Nor can it treat its material with the same spirit of observational detachment, for what is involved in speech about living, acting, and doing is simply the very stuff of our active engagements. Ethics is distinct by being a *practical* discipline. That is to say, it is concerned with good and bad reasons for acting.

The evolution of eighteenth-century Moral Science into the "Human Sciences" of the twentieth century brought into being studies of human action that conformed more closely to general scientific expectations. Particular human actions had become the material of the study of history; but now human action was interrogated for its recurrent patterns, the rise of Economics being, perhaps, the earliest and most striking fruit of this line of inquiry, followed in the nineteenth century by Sociology and Psychology. This evolution, however, left behind the original concerns of Ethics. The new sciences reported on how humans behaved as individuals and communities in response to circumstantial pressures, and proposed explanations for their responses, but always from the observer's, not the actor's point of view — a subtle nuance conveyed in the word "behavior." That meant that they never ventured upon the ground of *moral reason,* with its determinations of good and bad reasons for acting. The distinction may seem unimportant: it was a "Professor of Ethics," the journalists reported gleefully, who had "discovered" that businessmen behaved more cooperatively when a teddy bear was given a place at their table. But all the observation and explanation in the world for behavior patterns, individual and social, for desires, feelings, aspirations, values, norms, and so on, may include not a single word about *why* something should be done, or what is to be valued above what. The discourse of Ethics concerns ourselves, the life we are living, the action we have in hand. Even when pursued at a high level of reflection, it is of a different order from a discourse about patterns of behavior demonstrated in the past or probable in the future. "Ethics is not practical merely by having as its subject matter human action," wrote John Finnis shrewdly.[5] Something similar may be said about the newly recovered fashion for evolutionary accounts of moral thinking, such as those based on comparative neuroendocrinology which emphasize the role of the hormone oxytocin. Some "why?" is being asked and answered, to be sure. Some account is being given for ways in which we habitually feel and rule our feelings. But it is not the internal

5. John Finnis, *Fundamentals of Ethics* (Oxford: Oxford University Press, 1983), p. 3.

"why?" of the moral thinker; it does not inhabit the categories constitutive for moral thought. That means that such accounts have the effect of "knowing better," of describing moral thought away by situating it within explanatory sequences which bypass the questions and propositions that those who practice moral thinking for themselves might recognize.

But how does Ethics as a reflective discipline distinguish its inquiry from the projects of the moral thinker and the moral teacher? There is a commonplace way of making this distinction, which is too easy. Moral instruction, it is said, is normative, practically engaged with how we should act; Ethics is descriptive, reflecting in detachment on moral concepts and arguments. This is too rough, because moral instruction, too, reflects on moral thought; it corrects false understandings, not only bad behavior. And Ethics, while descriptive, is not detached; it reflects normatively.

A description of any thing must fit the reality of that thing, and a good fit can be verified only by holding the description accountable to the reality. What form of accountability can be offered for ethical description? It does not describe human *action;* if it did, it could be verified by observation. It does not describe what has been *thought* in relation to action, which could be verified by documentary evidence. It describes *trains of thought which resolve upon action.* But an account of how thought resolves upon action can be verified only by thinker-actors, and our only access to the thinker-actor is by reflection on moral debate and introspection into moral reasoning. Moral debate and reasoning are, by definition, normative. They are instances of moral thought, distinguishing good reasons for doing something from bad reasons and no reasons. A successful account of thought resolving on action, then, must be able to distinguish good reasons from bad reasons, as those who make these distinctions for themselves will recognize them. The normativity of the primary moral deliberation exports itself into the reflective analysis. We may grasp the point by thinking of how quotation marks can be used to distance a description of a debate from the questions raised in it. If we read that the Government urged realism, while the Opposition pleaded for compassion, we reckon we know what the debate was about. If we read that the Government urged "realism" while the Opposition pleaded for "compassion," the quotation marks, like sugar tongs, avoid direct mental contact with the categories, so we reckon we don't know what the debate was really about but only the terms in which it was conducted. This cannot be an account of the debate as those who conducted it understood it. No Ethics can fulfill its descriptive task by placing the whole of moral reason in quotation marks, distancing itself from the normative content of the categories.

Indeed, for most major contributors to Ethics the normative element has been the point of the exercise. They have aimed to describe not merely how people reason about moral questions, but how they *may* reason *well* about them. Reflection on moral reason does not stand apart from moral reason; it extends it in the direction of self-awareness and self-criticism, it refines its categories and perfects its reasonableness. In reflecting on thought towards living, acting, and doing, we own the living, acting, and doing that we think and reflect on, and, far from detaching ourselves, we invest ourselves in it more deeply. Ethics, as answerable to ordinary moral discourse and practice, cannot isolate the formal and limit itself to the logical relations of ideas. To abstract from moral categories and moral logic, the difference between good and bad reasons, the categories of right and wrong and good and evil, would be to abolish Ethics as an intellectual enterprise, and to settle back into history, social science, or journalism. Critically but sympathetically, ethical reflection takes up the categories of moral thinking, thinks alongside the moral thinker, not from a point of detached observation but normatively. If it objects to this or that exercise of moral reasoning, it does so because moral reasoning needs to be done better. In Ethics normative thinking becomes normative about itself.[6]

But here a danger arises: in its zeal to improve the quality of moral thinking Ethics can become programmatic, fastening on a single moment in the discursive processes of moral thought and constructing an account exclusively in terms of that moment. The opening sentence of the first section of Kant's *Grundlegung* is the paradigm instance of this zeal, so peremptory, so unqualified in its reconstruction of all our natural ways of thinking that it struck the mind of revolutionary Europe with the numinousness of a

---

6. This conclusion is not far from that of Alasdair MacIntyre in his account of the role of the moral and political philosopher in Aristotle. See his two essays on "Rival Aristotles," in *Ethics and Politics: Selected Essays,* Volume 2 (Cambridge: Cambridge University Press, 2006), pp. 3-40, especially p. 38: "Moral and political philosophy are to make explicit the nature of our directedness towards our ends and the function of various capacities and excellences in achieving them and so provide us both as agents and educators of agents with standards of justificatory argument. But those standards can never displace — indeed they presuppose — the standard of excellence provided for both agents and educators by the good human being." Neither is it far from the account of R. M. Hare, who suggests a three-way division of "morals," "ethics," and "descriptive ethics." Only the last is purely descriptive, consisting of factual reports on thinkers' views. Ethics, while reflective and critical, is still normative. See his "Ethics," in *Essays on the Moral Concepts* (London: Macmillan, 1972).

divine revelation, which unfortunately it was not.[7] Something very similar is afoot with Mill's "greatest happiness of the greatest number" principle, or, indeed, with R. M. Hare's employment of the Golden Rule. So there developed the fashion that anyone with an observation to make about a moral concept — H. R. Niebuhr's useful observations on responsibility, for example — had to present it in the form of a new moral program, an "Ethic of X," which proposed to drive its rivals from the field. Ethics became a Battle of the Titans, in which the rival *Grundmotiven* pitted against one another their capacity to save the appearances while reconstructing moral thought in terms of a single ruling idea. And as commonly happens with such battles, there was generated a secondary form of Ethics as a spectator sport, conducting a running commentary on the struggle from the sidelines: "Now the Utilitarians say this. . . . Now the Kantians reply . . ." etc. etc. In which stultifying form the educational cultures of Europe and North America, as though resolved to produce a generation more unfitted for life than any of its predecessors, imposed the teaching of Ethics (in place of religion) upon senior high school students. The battles were less real than computer games, their protagonists never more than two-dimensional reductions of a dense and complex moral experience.

How can Ethics justify its role as a reflective extension of moral reasoning? To many intellectuals in the eighteenth century there was no need for a Moral Science. The work of moral reflection could be carried on by intelligent literary instruction, through novels and *belles lettres,* which responded in *ad hoc,* improvisatory ways to the challenges of living. Our contemporaries, too, may often regard Ethics as an extravagant offering upon the altar of academicism. But the offering is needed — not to entrench morality in a university curriculum for its own sake, but to satisfy the requirements of moral reflection. For moral teaching lays claim to authority; a depiction of the moral shape of reality can hardly come out of the blue and commend itself on the strength of bare self-evidence. Its authority may be transcendent or immanent; it may depend on a revelation or derive from some tradition of wisdom; it may make its claim explicitly on the basis of community identity or prophetic proclamation or implicitly through the quality of its observation or the color of its language. But it cannot lay claim to *no* authority —

---

7. Immanuel Kant, *Grundlegung zur Metaphysik der Sitten* 4:393. The sentence was, of course: "It is impossible to think of anything at all in the world, or indeed even beyond it, that could be considered good without limitation except a *good will*." Trans. Mary Gregor, *Practical Philosophy,* Cambridge Edition of the Works of Immanuel Kant (Cambridge: Cambridge University Press, 1996), p. 49.

not while claiming to give practical direction! Since moral teachings differ and compete, if not totally yet over quite important matters, the question of authority will always arise. Furthermore, moral teaching demands thinking on the part of its disciples. "Hear, you who have ears to hear!" it calls to those who have to frame their own lives and take their own decisions. And since the disciple's thinking and deciding involves subjecting the teaching to inter-pretation, the question of how a decision can derive authority from a teach-ing will always arise. These questions Ethics is called upon to address.

In its double work of testing and proving, Ethics renders service both to those who think in order to act and to those who instruct others how to think in order to act. Moral thinking and moral teaching must be assessed both for adequacy to their context and for internal coherence. Moral thinking, moral teaching, and Ethics form a triangle of points of view through which reflection on reality and ordered reason are brought to bear on immediate practical discernment. In this triangulation Ethics by no means speaks the last word or establishes ultimate proofs. When Jesus says, "Your heavenly Father knows your needs before you ask," it is not for any reflective discipline to pronounce on the truth of the doctrine. God him-self must validate or invalidate it. What a discipline of reasoning can do, however, is explore the context in which such a statement about God may be made and believed: what natural theology or historical revelation may support or undermine it, what the conditions of its truth may be in the mouth of the one who spoke it. Or when some anxious soul is troubled by whether military service is compatible with the teaching of Jesus of Naza-reth, Ethics will not be able to bring these troubles to a resolution, but it can give them a reasonable structure, exploring and weighing the argu-ments by which conclusions on the one side and the other are reached, and so equipping the doubter to reach a resolution of his or her own.

Unlike moral teaching on the one side and Moral Theology on the other, Ethics makes no appeal, explicit or implicit, to authority. Yet it can know that *there must be* an authority for any moral teaching, and can per-form its own task on the assumption that such an authority is recognized. In this way it can be integrated into a confession of faith which is not itself a part of Ethics. We say, "it can," because we speak of it as an abstract, transferable discipline practiced in relation to sundry alternative tradi-tions of moral teaching. But since no practitioner of a discipline is that and nothing else, the "can" is a "must" from the existential point of view. The moral theorist has a life to live, and, like other folk, must decide on a sound basis for living. Though the practice of a theoretical discipline is over and above the practical conditions of life, it cannot be remote from them; the theorist must make assumptions for which the theory cannot vouch. Without such a point of reference beyond its own horizons Ethics finds itself retreating from life, driven back upon logical analysis and abandoning its normative pretensions, or (more probably, and worse) smuggling them in on the basis of dogmas it refuses to acknowledge.

Such a self-conscious positioning of Ethics within the wider convictions of Christian existence is undertaken within the discipline of Christian Ethics, or Moral Theology. Drawing on theological description it informs our understanding of the world we live and act in, and so re-shapes our moral thinking up to the threshold of action. As the Gospel speaks of conversion from darkness to light, from the worship of vain idols to the loving adoration of the Father of Jesus Christ, Moral Theology traces the ways in which conversion is mirrored in moral thinking and teaching. Its theme is not, we should note, a special *kind* of moral thinking, that of Christian believers, nor a special *kind* of moral teaching, that of Christian teachers. It has much to say about these, for they represent moral thinking and moral teaching become most truly conscious of themselves, but its theme is moral thinking *in general* and moral teaching *in general,* summoned by its own internal logic to be converted to God. Moral thinking is the vocation of Adam, an aspect of human nature. But Adam's vocation is never "pure" nature, conceivable in isolation and on its own, but is conceived only in the light of the Second Adam, who is Christ. And so Moral Theology draws out theological references already implicit in moral thought, which must be made explicit if morality is to succeed in directing our path through life. To that extent it has an apologetic task as well as a reflective one: it finds in human moral thought a ground for belief in the God who calls man to obedient self-disposal, and it makes that ground evident.

Does the name "Moral Theology" claim a *priority* for the theological aspects of its work over what it has in common with Ethics in general? We should be careful of false alternatives here. Conceptions of how Theology and Philosophy relate, derived, perhaps, from Kant's *Strife of the Faculties,* are not very successful when transferred to Ethics. As theoretical disciplines Theology and Philosophy may or may not develop independent interpretations of the universe at a guarded distance from each other, the one taking its stand on revelation, the other on reason, each knowing its limits and warned by the other as to where its competences cease — though even so this schema seems to suppose a philosophy in a systematic mold, more typical of Kant and Heidegger than of Wittgenstein. In Ethics, however, with its need to reach a concrete answer to the practical questions, the distance is not sustainable, and as neither discipline has proprietary rights, the contribution offered from any source, from Theology, Philosophy or any other discipline, will be valued simply in view of the light it actually sheds on the matter in hand. We should not be quickly frightened into thinking that Theology is somehow attempting to colonize Ethics and has overreached itself. Nor should we quickly assume that Philosophy offers a default position for a study of Ethics plain and unadorned. The proposition that Ethics needs to be done theologically is, I would think, a proposition to be held on philosophical grounds as well as theological ones. In different ways Philosophical Ethics and Theological Ethics both show themselves dependent: Philosophical Ethics, in that it is unable finally to resolve the alternatives it clarifies, Theological Ethics in its constant appropriation of categories that Philosophy provides, an interest that Philosophy does not reciprocate. Ethics needs Theology if it is to pursue its questions to a conclusion, while Theology needs a considered purchase on practical reason if it is to give an account of the regeneration of mankind by the life of God. Ethics is studied as Moral Theology simply because morality and theology are related concerns.

Philosophy is primarily a discipline of questioning, the very archetype of an academic study without an object of its own. That Philosophical Ethics is underdetermined, unable to reach moral conclusions of its own, is the verdict of its own most thoughtful self-interrogations. A formal critique of moral thinking needs to make contact with a substantive critique. Reflection looks both ways, measuring the adequacy of regulative moral thought against the coherence which the task demands, but also against the reality which is not ours to direct and regulate. Ethics cast exclusively in philosophical terms has an unfinished, loose-ended character. Moral Theology offers to complete it, not by giving final answers to unanswered questions or concrete directions in place of general principles, but by pointing beyond formalities of thought and language to realities that determine what answers are worth reaching. Yet even when studied as Theology, Ethics cannot afford to be without Philosophy.

Moral Theology and the Narrative of Salvation

What, then, does it require if Ethics is to be studied as Theology? In the first place, in the famous words of the Second Vatican Council, it requires to be "nourished on the doctrine of the Scriptures."[8] The question, which has agitated Protestant theology for some time without yielding a great deal of illumination, is what kind of use of a canonical and authoritative text can make Ethics well-nourished.

One must either say very much by way of answer to that question, or very little. Here we shall be content with very little, confining ourselves to two points of principle. First, Ethics reflects on the conditions of good moral *thinking*. Were it to posit an ideal relation of text to action which, in the name of obedience to scriptural authority, effectively abolished thinking, it would abolish morality, and thereby abolish itself. There is a necessary indeterminacy in the obedient action required by the faithful reading of the text. Acts are ordered in a basic repertoire of kinds and types, and of these kinds and types Scripture has a great deal of normative force to tell us; but Scripture does not determine the concrete act *itself,* the act we must perform *now*. If Scripture totally determined our actions, there would be no obedience, for there would be no deliberation. Deliberation does not simply repeat what it has heard; it *pursues* the goal of faithful and obedient action by *searching out* actions, possible within the material conditions that prevail, which will accord with the content of the testimony of Scripture. On the conditions of success in this pursuit Ethics as a theological discipline reflects. Those Anglicans between the Reformation and the English Civil War who took issue with the Puritan use of Scripture, did so in defense of faithful and obedient discipleship as they understood it. Hooker's advocacy of "reason," often misunderstood in later generations, saw it as a hermeneutic servant of the text, giving concrete deliberative form to the normative demand.[9] The same

8. *Optatam Totius, 13: "Specialis cura impendatur Theologiae morali perficiendae, cuius scientifica expositio, doctrina S. Scripturae magis nutrita, celsitudinem vocationis fidelium in Christo illustret eorumque obligationem in caritate pro mundi vita fructum ferendi."*

9. Richard Hooker, *Laws of Ecclesiastical Polity,* 2.1.2: "For whereas God hath left sundry kinds of laws unto men, and by all those laws the actions of men are in some sort directed; they (*sc.* the Puritans) hold that one only law, the Scripture, must be the rule to direct in all things, even so far as to the 'taking up of a rush or a straw'. About which point there should not need any question to grow . . . if they did yield but to these two restraints: the first is, not to extend the actions whereof they speak so low as that instance doth import of taking up a straw . . . the second, not to exact at our hands for every action the knowledge of some place of Scripture out of which we stand bound to deduce it, as by divers testimonies they seek to enforce; but rather as the truth is, so to acknowledge, that it sufficeth if such actions be framed according to the law of Reason; the general axioms, rules, and principles of which law being so frequent in Holy Scripture, there is no let but in that regard even out of Scripture such duties may be deduced by some kind of consequence."

point could be made without use of the term "reason": Donne, writing of the apostles' prayers in heaven for the church on earth, imagined that they were wholly concerned with the doctrine and use of Scripture:[10]

> As through their prayers thou'st let mee know
>   That their bookes are divine,
> May they pray still and be heard, that I goe
> Th'old broad way in applying. O decline
> Mee, when my comment would make thy word mine!

The two prayers the apostles are said to make, one for the church's doctrine of Scripture and the other for its use of it, are not contradictory. It is precisely *because* the apostolic writings are known as "divine" — the Jacobean poet does not shrink from the epithet, as later generations would — that "the old broad way of applying" is what is needed — "broad," not in the sense of being loose and indifferent, but exploratory and discursive. Scripture is the divine resource with which we confront the practical indeterminacy of decision. To short-cut the indeterminacy by over-prescriptive commentary would amount, in Donne's view, to making "thy word mine," substituting the peremptory determinations of church office — bishop, pope, General Assembly — or, indeed, of private opinion, for the divine word calling us to thoughtful obedience.

Ethics seeks to clarify the conditions of a faithful correspondence of action to text. What it does not seek to do is to *interpret* the text in practical terms. This misunderstanding prompts the familiar panic-stricken plea that we should not interpret Scripture "too literally." Perhaps, the plea suggests, unless we bind ourselves to the text with an elastic band rather than an iron chain, we may find ourselves ourselves bound to perform some impossible or incongruous act. But the panic is uncalled for. "Literal" is a category that describes ways of using words, and "literal interpretation" is one that supposes certain words to have been used literally. The authors of the Scriptures used words literally sometimes, figuratively at other times, as do we all; sometimes, indeed (and here lay the patristic insight that started this discussion off), they used a literal expression which *also* carried an intelligible figurative sense. The only possible answer to the question whether we should take the Scriptures literally is that we should take

10. John Donne, "A Litanie," 77ff., in *The Divine Poems,* ed. Helen Gardner (Oxford: Clarendon, 1952, 2001).

them literally when they are meant literally, figuratively when they are meant figuratively. In seeking to win ourselves an interpretative distance on the text, we are seeking either something we already have, or something we ought not to have. What we ought not to have is a formula for deciding in advance what the Scriptures shall mean, a general policy of interpretation which ensures against all risks. That is not reading. What we already have, on the other hand, and therefore do not need to seek in this panicky fashion, is the freedom to deliberate, to determine the course of action that will be most in accord with the teaching of the text. Moral thinking responds to the authority of Scripture with a deliberated and free action, and in no other way.

A biblical story, command, or counsel presents us with a train of moral thought, a discursive argument that runs, though sometimes we need exegetical insight to make it explicit, from some A to some B, led by its practical question, grounding itself on some principles of action, observing some contextual constraints and reaching some resolution. That whole course of thinking, from A to B, is laid before our attention as we seek to fashion a course of thinking of our own, from some X to some Y, led by our own practical question, observing our own contextual restraints, and finally reaching our resolution of the matter that is in our view. Between the Bible's course of thinking from A to B and our course of thinking from X to Y there is one great difference: the biblical story, command, or argument is closed, set firm within the text, not a matter for negotiation, argument, or contest; our course of moral thinking, on the other hand, is still open. Interpretation has to do with what is already the case about the meaning of Scripture; moral thinking is not about what is already the case, but about what is to be done next. Interpretative questions which bear upon the shaping of our testimony (for example, of how one passage should be read in relation to other passages, as when we read Jesus' teaching on divorce in the light of the Deuteronomic law on which it comments and the various apostolic applications that interpret it) are assumed to have been answered with sufficient clarity. Obedience is a matter of how our own confession is to harmonize with the testimony of Scripture, and it is concerned to achieve a correspondence between the *whole train of thought* of the text from A to B and the *whole* train of our thought from X to Y. We may express the relation in the formula $[A \rightarrow B] \rightarrow [X \rightarrow Y]$. Obeying the text's authority is not simply a matter of taking up the *conclusions* which its thought has reached, as in the formula $A \rightarrow B \rightarrow Y$, a literalism that short-cuts the task of obedient thought, $X \rightarrow Y$. Nor is it simply a matter of thinking *from the same principles* as the text, as in the formula A→X→Y, so that we overleap Scripture's exposition of what its principles imply, lifting the loosest and most generalized expressions out of their argumentative embeddedness to employ them as we will. In thinking, for example, about the possibility of divorce and remarriage in obedience to Jesus' teaching and the casuistic advice of Saint Paul, it will not be enough to shrink gratefully behind the complexity and variety of the textual witness, and improvise on the basis of some general principle which we claim to elicit from the Bible, such as, "God approves of lifelong marriage." Neither will it be enough to say, "Divorce and remarriage is forbidden by Jesus, and that is an end of the matter." *Why* it is forbidden, *how* it is forbidden, *what* is open and what closed by the prohibition — these are things the Bible would tell us within its own terms (which are those of the ancient world), in order that we may grapple with the tasks presented by our own pastoral situation. Nothing will count as "biblical" thinking but a careful correlation of the complexities of the one situation with the complexities of the other.

The second point of principle is that Ethics reflects on the conditions of obedience *to the realities which the Scriptures attest* — to those realities as a whole, that is, and not to selected parts of them which might seem specially apt for moral reflection. Obedience to Scripture can only be an exercise of faith — not, that is to say, faith *in Scripture,* but faith in the creating and redeeming work of God, to which Scripture bears authoritative witness. The idea is in fashion from time to time that what is needed is a "biblical ethics," in which texts of moral importance are sorted out from other texts, which are of purely dogmatic, historical, legal, or poetic interest, and pulled together under topical headings. The patristic church knew of such constructions as the pseudo-Augustinian *Speculum "Quis ignoret?"* — a work that purported to collect together all the commands of the Bible belonging to "moral law" as opposed to "ceremonial." Needless to say, such an exercise, even when extended beyond apparently prescriptive texts to include narrative or poetry, imports very definite presuppositions as to what will count as "ethical." It is a good test of those presuppositions in any case how much use is made of the Song of Songs and the imprecatory Psalms. It also, inevitably, flattens out the historical dynamic between the Old Testament and the New. The result is always flat and conventional, for such an exercise can only find in the Bible what it set out to find, echoes of its own presuppositions. A Moral Theology which constructs, or is constructed on, such ways of selective reading will be anorexic, rather than well-nourished. The Bible in Ethics must be the Bible — the testimony of God's appointed witnesses to God's work, in history, prophecy, law, poetry, narrative, theology, all of it capable of refreshing moral categories and re-focusing the task of moral inquiry, but only as it is allowed to have its proper place in its proper literary context.

One way in which this last point has sometimes been put has been to say that the scriptural character of Ethics must be mediated through its sister-discipline of constructive theology, Doctrine. I confess, I am myself reluctant to put it that way. The true point it intends is that between any particular text and the formed work of moral thought there is an overview to be taken, an overview of the role of the text within its wider textual set-ting and in the history of the scriptural revelation, which enables us to lo-cate the claim of the text on the practical questions before us. There may be, that is to say, something to be said as a whole about "politics in the Bi-ble," which must be kept in the back of the mind in any attempt to reflect constructively on the practical bearing of "Let every soul be subject to the higher powers." But just as we should hesitate to describe that something as a "biblical political ethics," which implies that we know how to extract it from the wider biblical message of the kingship of God, so we should hesi-tate to call it a "biblical political doctrine," for the same reasons. What it is is not so much the first stage in systematic or reflective thought as the last stage in reading, an intellectual activity that has its own capacity to survey the whole as well as peer at isolated texts. Both Dogmatics and Ethics, as systematic and ordered disciplines, depend upon that capacity to read at large. Yet, while not allowing that Ethics is *mediated through* Doctrine, it is important to insist on a proper *vis à vis* between Doctrine and Ethics. And here there is a Scylla and a Charybdis to be negotiated. Sometimes, espe-cially in the Protestant tradition, Ethics has not been distinguished ade-quately from the doctrinal disciplines. At other times — and this is the de-velopment the Vatican Council wished to correct — Moral Theology has operated in comparative independence of the truths which Christians be-lieve are supposed to shape their lives. We must comment briefly on each of these opposite temptations.

(a) The bracing Barthian war-cry, "Ethics is dogmatics, dogmatics ethics," seems to encourage the collapse of one into the other, but leaves it open which will swallow which. If some of Barth's own earlier observa-tions leaned to the view that all conditioned truths "stand within the brackets of the ethical question," the tendency of his school was to ignore the practical character of moral reflection and assimilate Ethics to Doc-

trine, reversing the nineteenth-century search of Ritschl and his followers for a moral "core" beneath the dogmatic "husks."[11] There is, of course, a sense in which all Theology is moral; something is certainly wrong with it if it does not lead into the practical reasoning that constitutes the life of the church and the believer within the church. Yet Dogmatic and Moral Theology must make their own discoveries, each going beyond what the other could have told it.

If, as a helpful fashion of recent years has maintained, Theology begins and ends in doxology, it cannot be refused its moment of exclusive attention to the being and working of God, *Te Deum laudamus!* in which the second-person pronoun comes to the fore accompanied by its predicate of divinity, while the first-person subject retreats into the suffix of the verb. What can and must be sung and said in praise of the Father of infinite majesty, his honorable, true, and only Son, also the Holy Ghost the Comforter, must be sung and said on its own terms. A Christology that could be cashed out wholly in terms of moral reason — Christ as the perfect exemplar of obedience or pioneer of human self-realization, for example — could hardly be adequate to the miracle of God's presence in human nature. There is an excess of divine action over human which can only be acknowledged and worshiped. But there is also something like an excess of human action, something not — or not yet — included in the announcement of God's being and works. When those who heard Saint Peter's sermon on the day of Pentecost asked themselves, "Men and brethren, what are we to do?" (Acts 2:37), it was a *next thing* that they asked about, not something they had already been told of in Peter's proclamation. There can be ways of framing doctrine which have had the effect of shutting the door in the face of that next thing, swallowing up the "what are we to do?" in the irrevocable gift and calling of God.

The complementary and non-exchangeable relation between them is clearly illustrated by the way each treats of sin. A duality in this idea has often been apparent since Augustine made the distinction of "original" from "actual" sin, the one the basis for our radical guilt before God, the other the effect of our humdrum day-to-day temptations. There is a third-person and a first-person point of view. As an objective reality, sin is a universal truth about mankind, a generic disunity with creation and a solidarity in refusal of the good. But sin is also experienced as a subjective reality, and in this light it

11. Karl Barth, *Ethics*, trans. Geoffrey W. Bromiley (Edinburgh: T&T Clark, 1981), pp. 63-66.

presents itself as "trial," a danger "crouching at the door" of every practical endeavor, but not a necessity, since to believe it so would be to renounce all responsibility for it. And this duality has been reflected in the way the two disciplines have handled it. One might say that Dogmatic Theology has stressed the *impossible universality* of sin, its significance as the defining qualification in the mis-relation between mankind and a holy God, where it has fallen to Moral Theology to speak of its *possible contingency,* to identify it as a horizon continually to be recognized and refused in each action that we undertake. Augustine expressed the two aspects in a paradox that perplexed his first readers: with the help of God's grace one may be wholly free from sin, if the will to be so is present; but with the exception of the Mediator himself there never was nor ever will be one in whom such perfection is attained in this life.[12] These are two aspects, not alternative or contradictory views. An age over-fond of grand cultural narratives liked to contrast "Hebraic" with "Hellenic" concepts of sin, radical guilt *(culpa)* with flaw *(hamartia)*. That was to confer false permanence on two moments in a dialectic relation. As soon as we try to think through the presuppositions and implications of either, we find it implies the other.

This example also illustrates what may go wrong when the complementarity of Dogmatics and Ethics is not sustained. What has tellingly been called the "collapse" of the doctrine of original sin in the eighteenth century was due to the false turn which early-modern Dogmatics had given it. Separating anthropological dogma from behavioral realities, treating the generic involvement in sin as a mere *propensity* or *predisposition,* it had reduced the thesis of universal sinfulness to incomprehensibility, and so demoralized the doctrine as a whole, promoting complacency and despair at the same time. The controversial attempts of Enlightenment and counter-Enlightenment thinkers — Kant and Kierkegaard, most obviously — to reconstruct original sin along subjective lines deserve more sympathy when we see them as attempts to restore an intellectual ruin, not to destroy a sound building.[13] The dogmatician, making sin exceedingly sinful, quickly resorts to apocalyptic largeness of scale. Sin is the refusal of God and goodness, Satanic and ultimate. Man's petty "no" to God is deep-

---

12. Augustine, *De spiritu et littera,* 1.1: *"ut sit homo sine peccato, si voluntas eius non desit ope adiuvante divina, et tamen praeter unum in quo omnes vivificbuntur, neminem fuisse vel fore in quo hic vivente esset ista perfectio."*

13. On their relation to the older tradition as well as on the wider problematic there is much to be learned from Wolfhart Pannenberg, *Systematic Theology,* vol. 2, trans. Geoffrey Bromiley (Edinburgh: T&T Clark, 1994), pp. 231-75.

ened by the Incarnation into a demonic "no," and sucked into the slip-stream of the Antichrist.[14] This is very fine, and every theologian will need at some point to follow this journey *via* the wastes of sin and the midnight sun of God's will in Christ to the pole where good and evil have their final confrontation. But a problem arises when the polar expedition has laid no plans for coming back again. If and when sin grows large in its scope, it assumes a demonic unity which forewarns of the flood at the end of time; but what are we to say about the many small streams of sin, the meanness of deficiency, the weakness of opportunity let slip, the inadequacy co-possible with every God-given possibility, which comprise what Paul called "grieving the Spirit"? Augustine did not make the mistake of confining sin to protology and eschatology. If his famous declaration that the beginning of sin was pride had an angelological content, inspiring, as is often said, Milton's depiction of Satan, his reflections followed a different path in respect of Adam and Eve, whose sin consisted in being deceived. In this he was alert to the New Testament Epistles, where the discussion of sin often looks in two directions: to protological definitions, on the one hand, taking sin back to a radically false position *vis à vis* the world and its creator; to broad phenomenological surveys, on the other, tracing the ways sin fans out into the variety of forms it assumes in the world.[15] And should we not go back even further, to Jesus' parable of the sower, with its three different ways in which the human heart may fail to receive the seed of God's word? Talk of sin must retain an exploratory, undefined character, for it is only as we discern the path of discipleship that we discern the ramifying possibilities of losing our way that lie open before our feet. That is the importance of Jüngel's valuable observation of the "pseudonymity" of sin, and of Pannenberg's remark that sin's true nature is "for the most part concealed. How else could it seduce us?"[16]

Behind both ways of collapsing the difference between Dogmatics and Ethics there lay the influence of Schleiermacher, who had characterized

---

14. Balthasar, "Neun Sätze zur christlichen Ethik," in J. Ratzinger et al., *Prinzipien christlicher Moral*, 4th ed. (Einsiedeln: Johannes, 2005), p. 78: *"Die Gegenwart der absoluten Liebe in der Welt vertieft das schuldhafte Nein des Menschen zu einem dämonischen Nein, das negativer ist, als der Mensch sich bewußt ist, und ihn in den Sog des Anti-Christlichen einzubeziehen sucht."*

15. On this I have written more in *The Ways of Judgment* (Grand Rapids: Eerdmans, 2005), pp. 78-83.

16. Eberhard Jüngel, *Justification*, trans. Jeffrey F. Cayzer (Edinburgh: T&T Clark, 2001), p. 95; Pannenberg, *Systematic Theology*, vol. 2, p. 252.

Christian Ethics as a description of Christian self-consciousness insofar as it took the form of an impulse to act. Though the distinction of Doctrine *(Glaubenslehre)* and Ethics *(Sittenlehre)* was maintained, both were rooted in a foundational religious theory which was neither Dogmatics nor Ethics but contained something of both of them: dogmatic, insofar as it took the form of a description of the church, ethical in that it concentrated on the spirit or ethos of the community rather than its outward form. From this starting point creedal and ethical reflection were to flow separately and equally. On the descriptive nature of the ethical enterprise Schleiermacher insisted. "Christian Ethics *(Sittenlehre)* can be nothing but the description of those patterns of action that arise from the prevailing influence of the Christianly defined religious self-consciousness."[17] Like any other descriptive discipline Ethics *follows* what it describes; it does not pretend to *produce* good actions. The idea of a normative discipline was, Schleiermacher thought, the essential mistake common to rationalism and Roman Catholicism. In Protestantism, he insisted, the imperative was replaced by the indicative.[18] There are, it is true, outright prohibitions which will be confirmed by a conscience duly formed by the reading of Scripture, but these are mere limit-cases. The positive task of Ethics is to describe (in general terms) all the activities of human life which are originated by the Spirit. What it describes is true only of the church, of the church only in normal, peaceful conditions abstracted from conflict, and of the church only in the modern, enlightened age. Such a description is closed, in that what it describes has in fact come to pass in history. There is no scope now for a deliberative inquiry into what is to be done.

One of the most striking features of Schleiermacher's outline is the place assigned to the person of Christ. "The beginning of morality is the perception of contradiction between old and new," and with Christ a new reality has entered human nature. Schleiermacher therefore took special interest in the correlation of Christological heresies with moral errors.[19] Yet there was not just one focal point in Christian Ethics, but two: the doc-

---

17. F. E. D. Schleiermacher, *Die christliche Sitte nach den Grundsätzen der evangelischen Kirche in Zusammenhange dargestellt,* ed. L. Jonas, 2nd ed. (Berlin: G. Reimer, 1884), 1.12.33. He continues: "*Indem wir aber sagen 'Beschreibung', so scheint darin selbst auch schon eine nähere Bestimmung der Form zu liegen, und noch dazu einer von der gewöhnlichen sehr abweichenden.*"

18. *Introduction to Christian Ethics,* trans. John C. Shelley, based on the 1826-27 lectures in the Peiter edition (Nashville: Abingdon Press, 1989), p. 62.

19. *Introduction,* pp. 107, 52-57.

trine of Christ, on the one hand, and the doctrine of the Holy Spirit on the other. Might not this acknowledgment, we may wonder, open the way for a deliberative inquiry in Christian Ethics? Schleiermacher refused that possibility. The Ethics of the Spirit, too, was purely descriptive, since it was subordinate to ecclesiology. "There is no need to say, 'You should, for the following reasons . . . ,'" he told us. "Nobody needs a motive except someone not yet in the Christian church."[20] The spirit of the community was "more primordial" than the division between thought and action. But did that mean that Christian Ethics was a merely historical science? Describing what has happened, it gives us no guidance, but if it directs what *is to be*, it is not descriptive at all, but normative. Schleiermacher resolves this dilemma by appealing to the power of description to excite imitation: when a depiction of the real relations and the ethos of the church is presented to us, the "living power lying within our perception" is awakened, so that we are inspired to conform to the pattern.[21]

Christian Ethics conceived as a purely descriptive discipline, we must fear, is incapable of accompanying moral reason from reflection to deliberation. Of course, a theological ethics is bound to be "realist," holding that our judgments on good and evil, right and wrong, are determined by reality "out there," something we have to *know*. In that it makes what God has done and said the ground of normative judgments, it casts itself on what is true about the world. Yet ethical realism cannot mean that the directive and regulative role of moral thinking is irrelevant or unnecessary. From statements about God as the ground of our action it must be possible to make the transition to how we are to live. Discipleship is not merely to be admired, but taken up as a task. A further difficulty in an Ethics conceived as *religious* description must be its silence about the ordered and structured beauty of the created world. A focus narrowed down to "the Christian life," i.e., to ecclesial piety and fellowship, appears to exclude the breadth, depth, and height of creation, the "world" with its proliferation of interrelated kinds and ends. There can be no objection, of course, to the idea that Moral Theology is a practice located within the church; the church is its form as well as its context, its questions are the church's questions, its answers accompany the church's life. But the church is not the object *about which* it raises questions, nor the presupposition on which it does so. Its "object" is simply its project, which is, how we are to think

20. *Introduction*, p. 87.
21. *Introduction*, p. 68.

about how we are to live; its presupposition is the word of God to mankind about his life.

(b) More briefly, what of the temptation on the other side, that of too great an independence of ethical from doctrinal thinking? This possibility surfaced especially within the tradition deriving from the pastoral ambitions of the Council of Trent, which envisaged Moral Theology as a kind of *ars gubernandi,* a regulative system for ordering the conduct of the faithful. A long tradition of critiques of "casuistry," of which Pascal's *Lettres Provinciales* was the earliest and finest example, as well as the fissuring of pastoral practice into rival schools ("rigorism," "tutiorism," "probabilism," etc.) bear witness to the tensions of pastoral practice when the goal of faithful discipleship comes to terms with the need for practical accommodation. It was a great pity that this critique, advanced with the most serious intent, was exploited in eighteenth- and nineteenth-century Protestantism to fuel a sullen anti-Catholic hostility.[22] The Second Vatican Council's call to re-found Moral Theology in a more biblical framework marked the point at which the Roman communion as a whole showed itself attentive and receptive to the concerns the critique had voiced.[23]

The common use of the term "casuistry" indicates a measure of confusion as to where the cause of offense lies. There can be nothing wrong as such with the rational ordering of cases under general rules; indeed, it is indispensable to ordered moral reasoning. We can hardly take seriously the complaint that in proposing a systematic exploration of types of moral dilemma the casuists were trying to forecast history. The problem lay rather with the directive pastoral ambitions with which the church took up the task of mapping moral cases. Pascal thought that pastors colluded with wrongdoing in offering resolutions for others' problems for which they bore no direct responsibility. Barth, while thinking the casuistic moralist arrogant in posing as an "ethical expert and a trustee," while placed "at a safe distance from the ethical battlefield like a staff-officer of the Lord,"

---

22. As a warning as well as an education, I keep on my shelf a book entitled *Awful Disclosure of the Iniquitous Principles taught by the Church of Rome: being extracts translated from the Moral Theology of Alphonsus Liguori, who was canonized in the year 1839, and of whose works the Papal Church has pronounced that they contain "not one word worthy of censure," with remarks thereon,* by the Rev. R. P. Blakeney, B. A. (Dublin: Curry; Nottingham: Deaden, 1846).

23. To what effect may be seen from such a striking example as that of Romanus Cessario, *Introduction to Moral Theology* (Washington, DC: Catholic University of America Press, 2001), esp. pp. 229-42.

agreed that "it makes it all too easy."[24] Both critiques are valid, though Pascal's is the more profound, for it is precisely the nature of a successful dictator to exercise control by kindness, arbitrarily waiving the strictness of the law to make managerial flexibility a substitute for principled conduct. The result was that Moral Theology could cease to be morally educative, and become, as Mrs. Kenneth Kirk is said to have described her husband's business, a matter of "finding arguments to justify what everybody knows is wrong." (It is, of course, a question for the historians whether the casuists of the seventeenth and eighteenth centuries, the pastors of the Reformed churches, the confessors to whom Alfonso Liguori addressed himself, and all who devised texts to guide pastoral counsel did their work rather better most of the time than these objections would suggest.)

Similar concerns, *mutatis mutandis,* were stirred by twentieth-century adventures which aligned Moral Theology with political agenda, whether of radical social change or of conservative resistance. In maintaining the distance between the reflective work of Moral Theology and an active political vocation, critics of this kind of political theology were no more saying that the church could do without political activists than critics of casuistry were saying that it could do without flexible pastors. The point was simply to preserve the *vis-à-vis.* The two roles must be constantly in conversation, the properly reflective, critical role of disciplined thought, on the one hand, and the free initiative of the agent on the other. Both are diminished by an attempt to fuse them; the activist cannot always wait upon the results of intellectual reflection, the thinker cannot iron out complexities in the interests of a practical programmatic simplicity.

Moral thinking itself is both directive and regulative. By it we conduct ourselves in response to what God has directed and regulated for us and on our behalf. Disciplined reflection on moral thinking cannot take the place of actual moral thought; it does not yield immediate directions for our conduct. It is normative, having in view the conversion of moral thought to reason and obedience, but its normativity relates to the way we think about what we do rather than to the concrete acts themselves. Moral Theology does not tell us, "Drop that gun!" It reminds us that murder is an offense against the image of God. Like political science, which confers political authority on no one but lends assistance to all who have political authority conferred upon them, Ethics affords normative wisdom to those

24. Karl Barth, *Church Dogmatics,* III/4: *The Doctrine of Creation,* trans. G. W. Bromiley, T. F. Torrance, et al. (Edinburgh: T&T Clark, 1978), pp. 11, 14.

who have undertaken to rule their lives under God's rule. It is a pastoral discipline, but a maieutic rather than a prescriptive one.

The two temptations, one to convert Ethics back to Dogmatics, the other to turn it into practical management, only arise because Moral Theology does in fact reach out in both directions, towards the doctrinal and towards the practical. It accompanies the course of Christian practical reasoning all the way from its apprehension of the truths of the creed to its practical discernment of the opportunities and duties opening up before its feet. That can be a considerable stretch. It is not surprising, nor in the least harmful, if there are books which the librarian is hard-pressed to know whether to place on the Moral Theology or on the Dogmatic Theology shelves. It is not surprising, and may be borne with good humor, when the moral theologian lecturing on just war or economic justice is asked sarcastically from the floor how long it will be before he gets to the theology. The danger is simply that Moral Theology may lose its reach, attach itself sluggishly to one of its poles, and through *always* singing the praises of God in heaven or *always* picking over the practical possibilities of action in difficult circumstances, may forget how to make the journeys of thought entrusted to it between heaven and the circumstances. It is in the movement between its poles that its peculiar vocation resides.

CHAPTER 5

The Task of Moral Theology

The Shape of Moral Theology

Talk of the conversion of moral thought in Christ may invite the wrong kind of expectations. It may seem to promise that, as new thought replaces old, grace-filled existence replaces natural morality, and the higher law replaces the lower, everything will become clear and unambiguous. The highest standards will be set, the transformation of human conduct will proceed unhindered, and we shall be free at last of the dreary compromises of this-worldly morality. With such perfectionist expectations projected on it, Moral Theology is bound to produce frustration and incomprehension. The expectations are wrong, and the reason they are wrong is that they fail to allow for the evangelical character of Christian thought, framed and animated by the proclamation of Christ and the promise of his Kingdom. An idealist Ethics overlooks what the Gospel has to tell about the nature of the present age. The age of Ethics is the age of discipleship, the age of anticipation, the age of the church, and the age of the Spirit, the age in which, as Augustine memorably put it, "our righteousness, too, . . . is in this life no more than forgiven sin."[1] Moral Theology, to speak evangelically, must speak of the world as we encounter it, for it is to that world that redemption has drawn near.

The implications of this may be explored from the magnificently architectural programmatic statement of the great unfinished symphony of the twentieth century, Karl Barth's *Church Dogmatics*, volume IV, *The Doc-*

---

1. Augustine, *City of God*, 19.27.

trine of Reconciliation, framed with his characteristic Christological focus. "The center" of the Christian message, Barth declares, is described "materially" as "God with us"; "concretely" it is spoken of by the name of Jesus. He it is who is "the center"; he it is in whom seven carefully measured steps of the doctrine of redemption have their concrete subsistence. These seven steps all have to do with divine and human action: God's being as act; God's action as event; the welfare of mankind as the saving history of God's action; the saving of mankind as the inner purpose of creation and history; the peril of man as the presupposition of salvation; the Incarnation as the accomplishment of reconciliation; and, finally, the determining of reconciled man as an active subject. Human action is the capstone of the arch in the reconciliation of man with God. "Not for us a passive presence as spectators, but our very own highest activation, quite simply the praise of the grace of God. . . . This 'we with God' implicated in the 'God with us' is Christian faith, Christian love and Christian hope; and these constitute the praise of God's grace that still remains for us to accomplish — still remaining as the essentially human thing, as the supremely important thing, as *action* in the truest sense of the word."[2]

If, then, we inquire how the agent is centered in him- or herself, competent and empowered, exercising freedom in self-identity, the answer can only be that the agent is centered also upon this absolute center, the moment of history at which the name "Jesus Christ" was made known for the redemption of the world. That moment was Jesus' resurrection from the dead. The idea of a "center" of history turns on what differentiates history from a mere extent of time, the narrative logic that underpins whatever has been undertaken or will be undertaken in time. The idea of a "center" of a human life turns on what differentiates an individual from a mere cross-section of the lifestream, the fitness of this human existence to that same narrative logic. With the self made sure upon that historical center, the agent is free to move in either of the two directions practical reason requires, towards world and towards time. The way is open in one direction from the empty tomb of Easter to the beauty and order of the life that was the creator's gift to his creation and is restored there. The way is open in the other direction from the empty tomb to a new moment of participation in God's work and being. (If we call these two directions "backwards" and "forwards," it will conform to the narrative logic which

---

2. *Die Kirchliche Dogmatik,* IV/1, §57.1, p. 14 (= *Church Dogmatics,* IV/1, trans. G. W. Bromiley, T. F. Torrance, et al. [Edinburgh: T&T Clark, 1961], p. 15).

places the empty tomb at the center, but we must avoid being misled by irrelevant suggestions that attach themselves too easily to these spatial metaphors. The sequence which places one moment behind and another before is simply that of the ordered purposes of God.) The risen life of the last Adam gives hope to the first Adam in the midst of God's created work. The risen life of the last Adam inaugurates the Creator's purpose to consummate all life, past, present, and future, in the reign of life. In the empty tomb we are shown heaven and earth, we are promised that they shall be restored, not destroyed and brought to nothing, and we are taught to look for new activity, new deeds, new possibilities that prepare the way for a new heaven and a new earth. These two directions are not alternatives, to one or the other of which Christian thought might equally well turn, adopting a "conservative" or a "radical" posture to taste. Neither are they sequential directions, that we should satisfy the demands of created order first and newness afterwards, like adolescents who must obey their parents and teachers until the happy day when, graduation certificates in hand, they are cast loose to encounter their own adventures. The two directions are mutually reinforcing angles of vision that depend for their intelligibility upon each other. Moral thinking is always descriptive of the world. Moral thinking is always opening towards the future. The bipolarity of value and obligation is irreducible.

An earlier volume of mine called *Resurrection and Moral Order* adopted an angle of vision that looked principally towards the objective order of created goods and the restoration of human agency by the resurrection of Christ. The importance of this view of things impressed me, and continues to impress me, in the light of the civilization's forgetfulness of created order, which persists, "green" issues notwithstanding, to the present day. The neo-orthodoxy that put Christ at the center without putting him *at the center of the created world* gave birth to an Ethics that danced like an angel on the head of a needle, wholly lacking worldly dimensions and focused solely on a conversion-encounter with the cross. The sublation of Ethics into faith, such as we find even in such an otherwise admirable figure as P. T. Forsyth, was founded on the simple assurance that the worldly content of Ethics was blandly self-explanatory and needed no interrogation, but only to be situated in relation to theology. A generation which saw the normalization of nuclear weapons and biotechnology could hardly sustain that assurance, unless with its eyes tightly shut. *Resurrection and Moral Order,* therefore, undertook to validate the interest of Theological Ethics in elucidating worldly order. What follows now may be regarded as a necessary complement to it, its angle of vision turned principally towards the subjective renewal of agency and its opening to the forward calling of God. The restored agent is also the renewed agent, filled with the life of God poured out within the world. In comparing the two books in this way, I speak only of their general directions. Much must be said here about the objective order of created goods; rather more was said there about the renewal of human agency than was apparent.

A friendly critic of the earlier book objected that with much to say about "moral order," it said too little about "resurrection."[3] Without discounting the thought that *Resurrection and Moral Order* did its work badly, we may, perhaps, see in this disappointed expectation an aspect of the resurrection itself. It directs our vision backwards and forwards, and does not let it rest where it is. The resurrection is a point of junction, where two angles of vision meet. We come, like Herbert's Easter worshiper, with "flowers to straw thy way," ready to welcome the recovery of life from death, but we find our flowers hanging useless in our hands as the risen Lord was ahead of us, "up by break of day."[4] So the three Marys' experience of the risen Lord was, first and foremost, the experience of an *empty* tomb, the negation of a negation, with no moral and spiritual dimensions of its own, an empty space, not void and meaningless, since it spoke of the overcoming of death, but full of the unknown and the unarticulatable, hopes and promises awaiting a future to give them form. The Gospel of Mark, as we have received it, ends (16:8) with the women appalled and silent at that unlooked-for emptiness. Then comes the angelic announcement of Jesus' risen life "going ahead," and after that the actual appearance; yet as they reach out to grasp its physical determination, they are told, "Do not cling to me! I am not yet ascended to the Father!" (John 20:17). And, finally, the risen Lord is taken into heaven, "goes ahead" to the end of time, an absence once again, yet not an empty one, but a space filled with the gift of the Holy Spirit. "Even though we once regarded Christ according to the flesh, we regard him thus no longer. Therefore, if anyone is in Christ, he is a new creation" (2 Cor. 5:16-17). The dimensions of the resurrection are what is to become of the form of the world: creation restored on the one hand, the creature led forward into new creation on the other.

3. Stanley Hauerwas, *Dispatches from the Front: Theological Engagements with the Secular* (Durham, NC: Duke University Press, 1994), p. 175.

4. George Herbert, "Easter," in *The Works of George Herbert*, ed. F. E. Hutchinson (Oxford: Clarendon, 1941), p. 42.

94

We can speak of creation restored, and have some imaginative idea of its content, referring to the form and order that is implicitly familiar and grateful to us. But how are we to speak of an eschatological elevation without being left gesturing, contentless, pointing towards indefinable and indescribable empty space? The characteristic way of Christian idealism has been to mark off one area of worldly life as a point of disclosure, where the heavenly life is revealed within the earthly. In the Middle Ages the "most perfect life" was held to be that lived by religious communities, and especially by the friars; in our own age theologians have claimed to find it sometimes in revolutionary political movements, sometimes in a church radically set apart, sometimes in martyrdom. It would be ungrateful to deny that the life of heaven may sometimes be revealed in such definite and determinate sites, but these observations, with whatever thankfulness they are made, report a miracle. They do not provide direction for the life we are called to live in obedience to what God has said and done for us. They cannot be converted into recommendation, counsel, or reproof. If not supplemented by *moral* reasoning, they confuse the task of existence with eschatological enthusiasm.

The way taken by the New Testament, on the other hand, is to speak of Pentecost, the life of the Holy Spirit poured out on all who believe and are baptized. Any complement, then, to my earlier attempt to write about the restoration of creation order in the resurrection must, in some sense, be about the Holy Spirit. Yet the Spirit, we are told, does not speak of himself. Talk about the Holy Spirit must all the time be talk about Christ, revealed, crucified, and raised from the dead. The resurrection is presupposed in the narrative of Pentecost; without Jesus risen from the dead there could be no pouring out of the gift from on high. "He led captivity captive, and gave gifts to men" (Eph. 4:8). But the connection runs in the other direction, too. Jesus was "vindicated in the Spirit" (1 Tim. 3:16), "demonstrated Son of God with power according to the Spirit of holiness by the resurrection of the dead" (Rom. 1:4). To talk about the resurrection is to follow after the risen one who has gone ahead, to step forward into the life of Spirit in which Jesus has been raised. The Spirit, like the Creator Father, veils himself, and as what we discuss in the ordinary course of business is, in the one case, the order of created goods, so in the other it is the ordinary practical impulses and movements of the human subject, but now heightened and drawn into the risen life of Christ, who is set before our eyes as goal and end to follow. What we find, as we turn our gaze forward, is not that we leave "old" forms of moral thinking behind, but that those forms of thinking are renewed, given back to us incomparably more disciplined, more informed, more comprehensive, more inviting, than they could have been before.

This does not mark a departure from the Christocentrism of mid-twentieth-century Barthian theology, but it does qualify it by adding a further strand. To what extent can we be thought to harmonize with its intentions? The signs may at first seem unpromising. Dietrich Bonhoeffer, notable as an exponent of the early Barth as well as being his own man, is apparently unwilling to see the Christ-event as vindicating any kind of existing moral thought. His essay "Ethics as Formation," written at the height of Hitler's military successes in the summer of 1940 and one of the fourteen or so fragments composed with a view to the never-completed *Ethics*, is memorable not only for its savage characterization of "the tyrannical men-despisers" who steal the vocabulary of community to dress up universal mistrust, but for a scathing portrayal in its opening pages of the traditional moralist as a Don Quixote tilting against windmills.[5] The throes of history which Bonhoeffer had to endure displayed, he believed, the bankruptcy of all Ethics: theoretical, systematic, rational, fanatical purist, the ethics of private virtue, of conscience, and of duty. Human moral reason is brought to nothing. In place of "abstract" and "casuist" ethics (alternatively, "theoretical" and "programmatic," two categories which include all the others) we have only the "concrete" ethic of the person of Christ, the form of man. In the central section, built with poetic power on the repeated use of the phrase *Ecce homo!*, Bonhoeffer explores the meaning of conformity to Christ through the moments of Incarnation, Crucifixion, and Resurrection. Conformed to the incarnate God we may be real human beings, not idealized pretenders to humanity; conformed to the crucified one we may bear the necessities of death and judgment humbly, not elevating ourselves above others; conformed to the risen man, we may live by virtue of a hidden source of life. The third section, still in pursuit of concreteness, speaks of the form of Christ "achieving form" through the living community of the church.

In seeking to understand Bonhoeffer's insistence on the "concrete" we must ask precisely what this polemic is directed against. Not against created humanity as such, nor against the powers of moral thinking that are native to it. Within the severe lines of his Christological framework

5. Dietrich Bonhoeffer, *Ethik*, ed. I & H. Tödt, E. Feil, C. Green (Munich: Kaiser Verlag, 1998), pp. 62-90.

Bonhoeffer felt perfectly free to speak of "natural" humanity and "creaturely" existence. Not against the transformation of human activity by Christ, for a "shimmer of the future" is said to mark the activity of the Holy Spirit in Christian lives in small ways, yet not so small but that the communal life of the church can be asserted as the proper form of it.[6] What the polemic is directed against is the sway exercised by intellectual constructs — the contentless categorical imperative of Kantian idealism on the one hand, the supposedly universal prescriptive provisions of Roman Catholic moral theology on the other. Both are unkindly portrayed by Bonhoeffer, but that is not the point. The point is simply that these two approaches are, for him, ways of failing to see the historical event of Christ as the nuclear core of the Christian life — one circumventing Christ in its confident definition of a universal norm, valid without historical conditions, the other, more complexly, treating him as an epistemic key to future challenges but sidestepping the ongoing presence of the Holy Spirit's guidance. "The concrete," then, is simply Bonhoeffer's way of demanding that saving history, with Christ at its center and the Spirit at its circumference, should be the matrix of all moral reason. That demand is, as such, unrefusable. We need only add the reservation that there never was a serious reason to fear that moral thought would turn out to be the exclusive prerogative of bad philosophy and bad theology. God's creaturely man and God's redeemed man have their own styles of creaturely and redeemed thinking-to-act; being conformed to Christ and not the world is, as Saint Paul tells us (Rom. 12:2), the renewal of the mind.

Faith, Love, and Hope

Awareness of self, awareness of the world, and awareness of time frame moral experience, not separately but interdependently, each affording a point of view upon the others. They structure moral reasoning, which moves among them intuitively and discursively on its path towards action. Theological moral reflection, too, which watches over the conversion of moral reason, is concerned with the recovery of a sense of self, world, and time. Recovered and converted, they form the structure of the discipline of Theological Ethics: "faith," "love," and "hope."

Ethics, to be sure, like any intellectual discipline, is a field of inquiry

---

6. Bonhoeffer, *Ethik*, p. 82.

encompassing many topics that can be explored on their own or in relation to neighboring topics. There are topics which concern the perennial features of the moral order of the world — topics like marriage or politics; there are topics which respond to the contingent challenges that life in the world may throw up at a given moment — topics like ecological responsibility or gender dysphoria; there are topics which concern the rational order of moral thought, such as prudence and faith. And to each topic its appropriate repertoire of concepts. For a comprehensive view of Ethics, too, there is a multitude of possible routes. Intellectual explorations share with other literary compositions the feature of singularity; no two treatments of the same ground will be quite the same. Yet in any reflective Ethics that knows its business the triad of faith, love, and hope will have a commanding place. The last word on the shape of Ethics can never be spoken, but that does not excuse a thinker from some predictable first words.

The Western Christian tradition has commonly taken a way into Moral Theology which, following the lead of Jesus' summary of the law, gives organizing priority to the concept of love: there is love of God, love of neighbor (in its various forms), and love of self, and perhaps also love of the world (both negative and positive). This approach has excellent precedent from Augustine onwards, and has enabled a great deal of importance to be said and thought about objective moral claims while escaping the false antinomy of duty and desire. But does it pay sufficient attention to subjective agency and to the questions of decision and action? Once it becomes important that one or both of these two complementary themes should be broached, there is a right and a wrong way to broach them. Neo-pagan concepts of "the will" and "history" are the wrong way; the right way is to speak of love, as the New Testament does, in conjunction with faith and hope.

Though the triad is most familiar from its use at the climax of 1 Corinthians 13, it was widely familiar to the church of the New Testament in the default sequence, faith-love-hope, which summarized the Christian life from beginning to end. The pair *faith and love* (in that order) is found in four texts (1 Thess. 3:6; Philemon 6-7; 1 Tim. 1:14; 2 Tim. 1:13), while two other texts associate them closely (Gal. 5:6; Eph. 6:23).[7] Longer lists in-

---

7. In Philemon 5 the order is reversed, but only momentarily and for rhetorical effect as "love and faith" are matched chiastically with "Christ Jesus" and "the saints" (the objects of faith and love respectively, as at Col. 1:4). The next verses, in a second chiasmus, place "faith" and "love" in the usual order again.

cluding the two, proximately and in the same order, occur at 1 Timothy 6:11; 2 Timothy 2:22, 3:10; and Revelation 2:19. The significance of the order is chronological: the Christian life begins with baptism (faith) and continues with participation in the community (love). When a third member is added, it extends the Christian life into continuing witness, especially in the face of persecution. "Faith, love, and endurance" are found in later New Testament texts, as a triad on its own or in a longer list, in four places (1 Tim. 6:11; 2 Tim. 3:10; Titus 2:2; Rev. 2:19 — the only relevant example outside the Pauline corpus), while "faith, love, and sanctification" are found once (1 Tim. 2:15; note also the sequence "love, faith, and sanctity" at 4:12).

When Saint Paul uses "hope" as the third member, then, it signals an attitude towards the passing of time. Of the four places where the triad occurs in the New Testament (1 Thess. 1:3; 5:8; 1 Cor. 13:13; and Col. 1:4), only the 1 Corinthians text, highlighting the preeminence of love, departs from the default order. In 1 Thessalonians 5:8, where the triad is married to a metaphor from military dress, faith and love come together to form a breastplate, while hope provides a helmet, suggesting that the first two are felt as a familiar pair. In the last of the four occurrences (Col. 1:4) Paul elaborates the conception as follows: faith is directed to Christ Jesus, love to the saints, and hope is "hidden in the heavens." In the earliest occurrence (1 Thess. 1:3) another explanation is offered: faith is a "work," love a "labor," and hope "patience." The outline is sufficiently well sketched: faith in Christ the foundation of Christian existence, love its social embodiment, hope its ground of endurance. Broadly, that will serve for 1 Corinthians 13:13, too, not least for the way the discussion of love is focused there upon the practices of community. That these three "endure" means that they form the permanent and invariable structure of the Christian life, as contrasted with spiritual gifts or attainments such as knowledge, which shall "pass away" — not only at the end of time, but in history. The preeminence of love, imposing a unique order on the three in this text, points to the crowning of action in community.

A true instinct, then, has led theologians back to these three when they have needed to clarify the connection between evangelical proclamation and the moral concepts of the life of faith. Augustine followed this way with his little "handbook" *(Enchiridion)* of the Christian life, as did Thomas Aquinas in his unfinished *Compendium*. Of many other possible examples I single out for notice some outstanding pages of William Tyndale, written as a prologue to his *Exposition upon the Fifth, Sixth and Sev-*

enth Chapters of Matthew (1532).[8] Faith, for Tyndale, is forward-looking. It is a "lusty courage and trust that we shall sin no more." In the light of some popular characterizations of early Lutheranism, what follows is surprising: faith in Christ's blood inscribes upon our hearts, Tyndale declares, the law as the chief object of our love. Love for the law means love for the order of reality disclosed through law, the order both of creation and of salvation-history. "To love the law truly, that is to say, to love God that is the Father of all and giveth all; and Jesus Christ, that is Lord of us all, and bought us all, with all our hearts, souls, power and might; and our brethren for our Father's sake (because they be created after his image) and for our Lord and master Christ's sake, because they be the price of his blood." Faith, then, is inseparable from love, because a sense of free and forgiven agency is inseparable from the objective universe of God, Christ, and neighbor. But faith and love together are inseparable from hope. "Faith, hope, and love are the inward baptism, and they are the mark of the true church. Where one of them is, there will be all three." They have their separate "offices": faith, to certify the conscience; love, to have compassion on the neighbor; hope, to comfort in adversity. Three offices, that is to say, within the practical attention of the Christian life: faith focusing the subject-agent; love embracing the world in its reality as the field of action; hope discerning the space of opportune time into which our resistance to adversity and our service to God and neighbor may be ventured.

To this example from the Reformation we add one from the twentieth century, Barth's use of the triad in the fourth volume of *Dogmatics*. Already in his early *Ethics* faith, love, and hope (in the default order, which he consistently adopts) had a major structural role; they corresponded to the command of God the Creator, the command of God the Reconciler, and the command of God the Redeemer. These three forms of divine command required, respectively, order in relation to life, humility in relation to law, and gratitude in relation to promise, and were mediated by vocation, authority, and conscience.[9] A quarter of a century later Barth abandoned the trinitarian way of distributing the theological virtues for a wholly Christological one. The person of Christ in his threefold office as king, priest, and prophet imposed the triadic structure, to which scheme Barth

---

8. William Tyndale, *Expositions of Scripture and the Practice of Prelates*, edited for the Parker Society by Henry Walter (Cambridge: Cambridge University Press, 1849).

9. Karl Barth, *Ethics*, ed. Dietrich Braun, trans. Geoffrey Bromiley (Grand Rapids: Eerdmans, 1981), p. 61.

assimilated the divine and human natures and the one person of the Chalcedonian formula — how successfully, we need not here decide. This Christological triad yields a threefold form of sin — pride, sloth, and false-hood — and a threefold remedy for sin — justification, sanctification, and vocation. This threefold work of the Spirit takes effect both for the believing community and for the individual believer: for the community in the forms of gathering, upbuilding, and mission, for the believer in faith, love, and hope.

What are we to say of this striking construction? We cannot fail to notice one or two stress-cracks. What a disparate jumble of themes occupies the third place in the various triads — the unity of Christ's person, his prophetic witness, the sin of lying, Christian vocation! Can they cohere to yield an exposition of the meaning of hope? And by what conjuring trick do faith, love, and hope come to be focused exclusively on the *individual subjectivity,* as "acceptance," "self-surrender," and "expectation"? With the fragmentary fourth part-volume, which should have presented the "special ethics of reconciliation," the surprise grows greater. Here Barth forsakes the triad of faith, love, and hope entirely, replacing it with an account of the Christian life as invocation traced through the Lord's Prayer, framed (in what must be the most perplexing decision of the whole *Dogmatics*) by two essays on the sacraments of baptism and Eucharist, supposedly a "prologue" and an "epilogue" to Ethics.

So faith, love, and hope do not, after all, occupy a place in Barth's account of Ethics. As volume IV of his *Church Dogmatics* launched out from the dry land of dogma the theological virtues were left like unemployed pilots sitting with their legs dangling over the harbor wall and gazing out to sea, when they might have been guiding shipping through the straits of moral reason. Why? We can only suppose that they fell victim to the author's persistent nervousness of general moral principles which would be applied to actual cases discursively. The underlying concern was respectable: he wished to protect the practicality of moral reason from what he saw, polemically, as philosophy's determination to reduce it to transcendental theory. But it gave a persistently punctiform character to his account of ethical responsibility, repeatedly characterized in terms of *this* agent's being commanded to do *this* thing at *this* moment. The result was a collapse of the discursive character of moral reason and, consequently, the loss of its relation to the truths of doctrine, so that the structure of Barth's ethical tracts rests in fact on a far narrower base than the generous contents of the dogmatic tracts and the bold program, "Ethics is dogmatics,

dogmatics ethics," would lead one to expect. Theology's role in accompanying and illuminating the believer's lived faith was constricted, and the role of faith, love, and hope as bridge-concepts between Doctrine and Ethics was constricted accordingly.

To perform their conceptual function, faith, love, and hope must be located both in relation to the final *perfection* of mankind and the conditions of *natural* human activity. The scholastic habit of referring to them as the "theological virtues" took its bearings from perfection, differentiating the three from the four natural, or "cardinal," virtues of prudence, temperance, fortitude, and justice. As Saint Thomas explains it, we have a twofold end, or perfection: to achieve the full potential of our human nature, and to be admitted to participation in the life of the godhead. These three virtues have God as their object; only he can impart them to us, and only in Holy Scripture can they be learned of. The order adopted by Saint Paul in 1 Corinthians is therefore valid once and for all: faith has priority in the logic of their generation, love in the logic of their perfection.[10] And yet, we must add, they cannot be so wholly distinct from the virtues of natural humanity as to suggest that nature is replaced, rather than perfected. Certain natural and theological virtues which apparently belong together — courage with faith, judgment with love, prudence and temperance with hope, etc. — become perilously separated in the scholastic treatment, while hope fares badly when cut off from our worldly experience of the opacity of future time, attracting only six questions in the *Summa Theologiae* compared with sixteen on faith and twenty-four on love.

Natural moral experience takes shape as a threefold awareness, we have said, and moral reasoning as a movement among the three poles of attention — self, world, and time. This pattern is taken up and enhanced in the redemption of the moral life. Here the logic of the default order, faith-love-hope, reasserts itself, with love presupposed by hope as reflection is presupposed by deliberation, and faith presupposed by both of them. Faith anchors the moral life in an awareness of self and responsibility, for agency is disoriented and uncertain until we grasp hold of God's work in shaping us to be effective agents. Love structures our awareness of the world and our appreciation of its ordered values, rejoicing in the world as God's creation and its history as the stage of God's self-disclosure. Hope focuses our awareness of time upon the "works prepared before us to walk in" (Eph. 2:10). Within these three perfections we find all else — and there

---

10. Thomas Aquinas, *Summa Theologiae,* 2-1.62.

is much else — that is important to moral awakening and moral thinking. They are a triad, mutually formative and mutually interpretative, each perfecting our lives in relation to the other two. We must not fall short of Saint Paul's assertion that they "abide — these three." Their unity can be expressed by saying that the gift of *self,* perfected in faith, provides a point of view from which we may understand the *world* as affording us *time to act;* the gift of the *world,* perfected in love, provides a point of view from which we may understand the *self* as laying claim to *its own time;* the gift of *time,* perfected in hope, provides a point of view from which we may understand the *self* as active *within the world.* And yet there is something else that is not to be lost sight of: Paul's famous dictum that "the greatest of these is love," correctly understood by Thomas as belonging to the logic of perfection.

We conclude this induction into Ethics as Theology, then, with a journey through the trajectory of this sequence, tracing how the active self expands into loving knowledge, is narrowed down to action, and finally attains rest in its accomplishment. To a second and third part we postpone a more leisurely exploration of these stages on action's way.

CHAPTER 6

The Trajectory of Faith, Love, and Hope

The Root of Action

We should not look for an "essence" of morality either in faith or in love or in hope. Moral reasoning follows a trajectory from one to the other. Morality is self-determination, but not essentially self-determination. It values objective goods, but is not essentially evaluation. It looks forward, but is not essentially a project for the future. Moral reasoning is realized only in a dynamic interplay of faith, love, and hope. "Because the one is known by the other," wrote Tyndale, "it is impossible to know any of them truly, and not be deceived, but in respect and comparison of the other."[1] Yet there is a dramatic order of origination to be observed: faith *anticipates* hope and love, but hope and love *presuppose* faith.[2] Self, world, and time are all gifts of God, but world and time could not be gifts *to us* unless we were first given to be agents fit for world and time. "Faith is the life of man," comments Tyndale, "*out of which life* the pleasantness of all his works spring."[3] And so the theological tradition assigned faith a certain priority: the prior giftedness of the active self — not an achievement of our dealings in world and time, not a chance by-product of the accidents of world and time — makes faith the first moment of divine grace. Faith cannot appear in the middle of the sequence, thrusting itself between world and time, which would produce

1. William Tyndale, *Expositions of Scripture and the Practice of Prelates*, ed. Henry Walter (Cambridge: Cambridge University Press, 1849), p. 13.
2. Augustine, *Enchiridion*, 2.7f.: "*Fides credit, spes et caritas orant. Sed sine fide esse non possunt. . . . Porro aliquid etiam quod non speratur, credi potest.*"
3. Tyndale, *Expositions of Scripture*, p. 125, italics added.

something like the transcendental philosophy of Kant, in which the agent rises above the world before engaging with it. Yet the priority of faith is antecedent; it is not a primacy or preeminence. Preeminence, if we follow Saint Paul, can be ascribed only to love. In the Kingdom of Heaven faith will not crown love and hope, but love will crown faith and hope. Faith precedes love as its herald, and cannot be spoken of except in an orientation towards love, which binds us to objective reality, and through love towards hope, which endures to accomplishment.

We may properly describe faith, then, as the "root" of morality. The author to the Hebrews, in presenting his famous rehearsal of the accomplishments of Israel's heroes, introduces it with the declaration that faith "gives substance to the objects of our hope and proves realities that cannot be seen" (11:1).[4] That is to say, faith gives rise to action by opening the self to the prospect of its own fulfillment in the objectivity of reality. Fulfillment is not merely what comes next in time; reality is not merely what appears to the senses. They are what faith grasps as the condition of its own active unfolding. In reaching past *first* appearances of reality and *immediate* anticipations of the future to see the secret of the world and time, faith is not an immanent human power but an operation of God himself. In this sense we understand the forbidding warning that without faith we cannot please God. "Whatever is not of faith, is sin," we are told; if we eat without faith, we are damned if we eat (Rom. 14:23). For faith is absolute, allowing no more or less, no gradations between faith and unfaith. One step is everything. "If you had faith as a grain of mustard seed . . . ," says Jesus (Luke 17:5-6). It is either present or absent, and to ask for an "increase" of faith is a category mistake.

So Jesus understood it as his calling to elicit faith in response to the presence of God's kingdom. He looked to "find" faith, as in the case of the centurion at Capernaum (Matt. 8:10; Luke 7:9), and in a saying known to Luke, "When the Son of Man comes, will he find faith on earth?" (Luke 18:8). With the bearers of the paralyzed man (Mark 2:5 and parallels) and

---

4. This statement is not rightly understood as a *definition,* a mistake which has corrupted all strands of the English translation tradition. The New English Bible first introduced the gratuitous words, "And what is faith?" immediately before it, while the Revised Standard Version, looking for a subjective term to define a subjective state, rendered ὑπόστασις as "assurance" (misled, it must be said, by good authorities; cf. W. Bauer, W. Arndt, and F. W. Gingrich, *Greek English Lexicon of the New Testament*). Who, I wonder, has raised the status of this verse as a definition since the subtle and discriminating discussion of Thomas Aquinas (*Summa Theologiae* 2-2.4.1), which has unfortunately been ignored.

with the Canaanite woman who begged for her daughter's cure (Matt. 15:28), he found faith in the bold persistence of a demand made on himself. "Your faith has saved you!" he said, or "Be it done to you as you have believed!" attributing his miracles to the faith of those who sought healing for themselves or others (Matt. 8:13; 9:28-29; Mark 5:34 and parallels; 10:52; Luke 17:19; 18:42). Exceptionally, as no illness was involved, the same words were addressed to the sinful woman at supper, in whose open display of love and grief Jesus saw evidence of faith (Luke 7:50). In his teaching about miracle he spoke of faith as the seed of the mustard tree, so small as to be almost without a place in the world but vast in its potential, capable of expanding and accommodating a great variety of creatures (Matt. 13:31-32; 17:20, and parallels). He rebuked anxiety as lack of faith; the story of the calming of the storm (Mark 4:40; Luke 8:25) is an occasion for Matthew to put a favorite epithet upon his lips, *oligopistoi*, "small-faithed" (Matt. 8:26), which also serves the story of Peter walking on the water (Matt. 14:31).[5] At the last supper Luke represents Jesus as praying for Peter's faith (Luke 22:32), which will be seen in his conversion after failure and his subsequent service to the church's stability.

It was the great work of the Reformation to recover and reassert the priority of faith as the root of action. Formally, this breakthrough was made possible by setting aside the scholastic classification of faith, following the Aristotelian distinction, as an *intellectual* virtue. For Saint Thomas faith was a "habit of mind" *given form in act* by love, which is to say, the intellective state *preceding* the motion of an appetite: "Without first apprehending its object by sense or intellect, the appetite cannot move towards it in hope or love. Faith is how the intellect apprehends the object of its hope and love."[6] Thomas's conception went back to Augustine's *Enchiridion*, where we are told that new believers were taught the creed under the heading of Faith, the Lord's Prayer under the headings of Hope and Love. Here the priority of faith is clear enough, but faith is removed from the sphere of action; it comes first because it is an act of knowledge, and no more. From which it follows for Augustine that love and hope can only be directed to goods, but faith has "bad objects as well as good."[7] Faith may

---

5. Saint Luke, too, can use the word, as at Luke 12:28; cf. Matt. 6:30.

6. Thomas Aquinas, *Summa Theologiae*, 2-2.4.2-5; 2-1.62.4: *"Non enim potest in aliquid motus appetitivus tendere vel sperando vel amando, nisi quod est apprehensum sensu aut intellectu. Per fidem autem apprehendit intellectus et quae sperat et amat."*

7. Augustine, *Enchiridion*, 2.7: *"Est itaque fides et malarum rerum et bonarum, quia bona creduntur et mala."*

join forces with love and hope; but it may make common cause with regret and resentfulness, as in the case of the devils who according to Saint James "believe and tremble" (2:19). Faith, in this exposition, is bare assent, not yet associated with the glad consent of the affections. To which the Reformation replied, correctly, that the proper object of faith is God, in whom truth and life are indivisible. His truth *per se* quickens and activates. That faith is "formed" through love is not in doubt — the formula goes back to Saint Paul himself (Gal. 5:6) — but that is not because faith is inactive, but because its active power is undetermined and unworldly until it is given an object to focus upon in love.

This was an important element in what the Reformers meant by their contested doctrine, "justification by faith." If one side of that doctrine lay in Luther's demand for "separation" and "distinction" between a "passive" realm of the transformed conscience and the realm of action, the other lay in the renewal of human agency, the restored identity, coherent purpose, and confidence of the human subject who could "descend from heaven and fructify the earth like rain," as Luther's own colorful analogy put it, plunging into works of justice and charity, seizing on the tasks that came to hand.[8] To recall the grand passage from the 1522 *Preface to Romans:* "Oh it is a vital, active, busy and effective thing, this faith! Impossible it should not incessantly be doing good!"[9] This rediscovery of active faith soon became the common property of theologians on both sides of the great church division, not a Protestant prerogative alone. If, as has been argued many times, the Church of England and the Council of Trent were not far apart on the question of justification, that is because the question of renewed agency was, in different ways, central to both their treatments of the subject.[10] The expression "faith only," or "faith alone," frequently enough, of course, obscured the essential point; what was meant was that faith *preceded* love and hope, not that it could do *without* them.[11] If there was one

8. Martin Luther, *Commentary on Galatians*, Argumentum (*WA* 40(1).51): "*Hanc cum intus habeo, descendo de coelo tanquam pluvia foecundans terram, hoc est: prodeo foras in aliud regnum et facio bona opera quecunque mihi occurrunt.*"

9. Luther, *Preface to Paul's Epistle to the Romans* (*WA*, Deutsche Bibel 7.10): "*O es ist eyn lebendig, schefftig, thettig, mechtig ding umb den glauben, das unmüglich ist, das er nicht on unterlas solte guts wircken.*"

10. See Henry Chadwick, "Justification by Faith: A Perspective," in *Tradition and Exploration: Collected Papers on Theology and the Church* (Norwich: Canterbury Press, 1994), 93-134.

11. As observed long ago by Richard Hooker, "A Learned Discourse on Justification": "Our fathers might hold, We are justified by faith alone, and yet hold truly that without

point on which everyone in the Reformation controversies agreed, it was that "faith without works is dead" (James 2:17). Faith is nothing if not the subjective root from which a life of active love proceeds: "Faith in Christ first certifieth the conscience of the forgiveness of sins . . . and then bringeth the love of God and of his law into the heart."[12] It is the awareness of the self made competent by an act of God to overcome the incompetence of guilt and self-doubt — not an accompaniment to love and hope, not a complement to them and certainly not their product, which would be the "faith of works," the target of the Reformers' polemics.[13]

Justification by faith is one of a family of moral doctrines that conceive the moral value of human action not simply as a function of its external performance, but in terms of a certain inwardness, a disposition which authenticates it as the true expression of an agency. What the Reformers maintained was that human action could be the object of God's pleasure, and so deserve the epithet "good," only if it expressed a deeper active impulse from which it sprang "necessarily." All doctrines of this family teach, in one way or another, the need for human action to be "sincere," which is to say, for the outer and the inner to line up, the outer expressing truly what the inner conceives. Where they differ is in how they understand the inner side of action. Is it "motive," or "will," or, as for Eliot, "reason"?[14] Justification by faith, uniquely among this family of doctrines, escapes the subjectivism of the idea that sincerity is a matter of the agent's unity with him- or herself. The inner reality from which the outer act must spring is at the same time the *subjective* root and the *objective* ground of agency in God's own act. Good action expressed, beyond and behind the agent's self, the supremely objective action which determines the reality of the world we live and act in, which is God's own action. Good works were "pleasing and acceptable to God," they held, "in

---

good works we are not justified." *Works*, ed. John Keble (Oxford: Oxford University Press, 1841), vol. 3, p. 508.

12. Tyndale, *Expositions of Scripture*, p. 88.

13. Tyndale, *Expositions of Scripture*, p. 14: "If you say, Seeing faith, love, and hope, be three virtues inseparable; ergo, faith only justifieth not: I answer, though they be inseparable, yet they have separable and sundry offices. . . . Faith only, which is a sure and an undoubted trust in Christ, and in the Father through him, certifieth the conscience that sin is forgiven."

14. T. S. Eliot, "Murder in the Cathedral," pt. 1, in *Complete Poems and Plays* (London: Faber & Faber, 1969), p. 258: "The last temptation is the greatest treason: To do the right thing for the wrong reason."

Christ," which is to say, in the context of what God had done for human agency in the crucified Redeemer.[15]

One effect of the Reformers' emphasis was to prevent what moderns have come to call the separation of fact and value — the polarization of cognitive thought and the active impetus. A profound opposition of the true and the good could never provide a basis for agency. Theoretical reason terminates in truth, practical reason in a resolution to act. The distinction, however, is modal, not metaphysically fundamental. Faith is both receptive and active. Another effect was to free agency from enslaving dependence on other worldly agents or objects. If agency cannot rest on cognition, neither can it rest on an energy supplied by attraction. That is why we speak of "justification by faith" and not "justification by love."[16] There is, of course, as good a precedent for the application of the metaphor of the root to love as there is for its application to faith. But a metaphor is as good or as bad as what is said by it, and what must not be said by speaking of love as a root is either that agency is the product of the working of other created beings upon us, or that it is an immanent and independent energy within ourselves, the modern "will." Within an evangelically conceived practical reason justification is by faith alone because the root of our human action is the objective act of God alone, summoning our agency into being.

In their reformulation of the tradition the Reformers were, of course, drawing on elements already present in it. When speaking of faith as cognitive, Augustine and Aquinas were careful to indicate that this was only an *incipient* cognition, an apprehension of truth, not a full grasp of it. Faith is not knowledge, but knowledge-minus, a cognitive orientation towards realities that are still uncertain and unclear.[17] Faith concerns "things not seen," and precisely for this reason, Augustine tells us, it is a practical trust in what appearances testify. Existentially, we owe faith to God's good

15. "Articles of Religion" 12: *Of good workes.* "Albeit that good workes, which are the fruites of fayth, and folowe after justification, can not put away our sinnes, and endure the seueritie of Gods iudgement: yet are they pleasing and acceptable to God in Christe, and do spring out necessarily of a true and liuely fayth, in so muche that by them, a lyuely fayth may be as euidently knowen, as a tree discerned by the fruit."

16. The proposal of Karl Rahner, challenging Hans Küng's Catholic appropriation of the Barthian doctrine of justification: "Questions of Controversial Theology on Justification," *Theological Investigations* 4, trans. Kevin Smyth (London: Darton, Longman & Todd, 1974), pp. 189-218.

17. Thomas Aquinas, *ST* 1-2.62.3: *"minus virtute, cognitio imperfecta."*

world, as we would owe it to a friend to repose trust in his good will.[18] Faith is both active, "working through love," and in anticipation cognitive, "reaching out towards sight."[19]

And if it is true that faith is a capacity to recognize "bad objects as well as good," this indeterminacy is not a kind of cognitive detachment. Scientific knowledge is cognitively detached, not because it is prior to commitment but because it has suspended commitment. Faith's indeterminacy is different; it is the moment *before* the determination of knowledge as love and of love as knowledge, the moment which issues in a grasp of what is real enough to be known in love. Suppose I am told that something dreadful has happened — let us say, a terrorist outrage in which large numbers of innocent people have been killed. On first hearing of it my knowledge can only take a provisional form, that of belief mingled with unbelief, an affirmation of what I have heard which is at the same time a question. I hunt around for whatever may make the report digestible and rescue the world I dwell in from the reign of moral contradiction. I may find this redeeming feature in a work of God, I may find it in some instance of human courage at the scene, I may find it in the sour reflection that the victims' complacency deserved, after all, to be shattered so that cosmic justice has been upheld. All these provisional ways of "coming to terms," as we call it, were plentifully in evidence in the wake of September 11, 2001. We settled for one or more of them, or else we banished the event from our minds as soon as we could, and got on with life as though we knew nothing — coming to terms without coming to terms. Coming to terms is a work of faith; it means reaching out for a form of things to love within the confusing half-realities presented to us. One way or the other, we were bound to look for a formal object on which a stable affective knowledge could rest. The implication of hating what we suppose to be the case is refusing to accept that it really is the case, and so ceasing altogether to believe. The devils believe and tremble, but they are, after all, angelic beings held in the suspension of the paradox, an eternal sign of the contradiction of sin. We humans do not believe and tremble for very long; the longer we tremble, the less we believe. Our faith is self-appropriation and self-donation in knowledge, reaching to embrace the truth of the world as it has been shown to us. In being offered truth, we are offered a grasp of ourselves as knowers and do-

18. Augustine, *De fide rerum quae non videntur*, 3f.

19. Augustine, *Enchiridion* 1.5: "*Cum autem initio fidei quae per dilectionem operatur imbuta mens fuerit, tendit bene vivendo etiam ad speciem pervenire.*"

ers of the truth. It is a moment of freedom, but *for* the world and *for* the moment of time. World-hatred is often a posture put on for show. If it is real, it means the end of us as agents, for freedom exercised against the world and time subverts the conditions of its own emergence, and destroys itself.

So we see how the classical account of faith as knowledge must, to the extent that it understands itself, develop precisely in the direction that the Reformation took it, to a "passivity" of faith that is not inertness or disinvolvement, but, as Luther himself continually explained it, receptivity and openness.[20] The Council of Trent, indeed, found its own way of looking in that direction when it identified "the beginning of justification" with an experience of being summoned, which leaves man receptive but "not utterly inactive."[21] The great "distinction" Luther would make between active and passive righteousness was not a distinction between what we do and what we learn about, but between a righteousness we perform and a prior righteousness of which we gladly allow God's performance in and for us. That is the force of the saying, "Faith comes from the hearing" (Rom. 10:17). The root of agency lies not in self-perception, but in receiving God's address to us. That does not make it the slightest bit less practical. Passive-receptive faith is not theoretical reason. It is the consciousness of being called to life by God, who tells us of our agency by telling us of his.

Love and the World

Not called to life in a vacuum but to life in the world, we are called, therefore, to know and love the world. "Does not wisdom call?" That is to ask, does not the order and loveliness of the created world call us to know it and love it? Does it not call us to recognize it as the work of a Creator, the

---

20. See, for example, Luther's *Commentary on the Epistle to the Galatians* (1535), Argument (*WA* 401.40f.): "*Est iusticia quam nos facimus, sive fiat ex puris naturalibus, sive etiam ex dono dei, quia ipsa iusticia operum est quoque donum dei, ut omnia opera etc. Sed iusticia quae ex nobis fit, non est Christiana iusticia, non fimus per eam probi. Christiana iusticia est mere contraria, passiva, quam tantum recipimus, ubi nihil operamur sed patimur alium operari in nobis scilicet deum. Haec non intelligitur a mundo: 'In mysterio abscondita' etc.*"

21. *Decretum de Justificatione* (sessio VI) 5: "*justificationis exordium . . . praeveniente gratia sumendum esse, h.e., ab ejus vocatione, qua, nullis eorum existentibus meritis, vocantur . . . ita ut, tangente Deo cor hominis per Spiritus Sancti illuminationem, neque homo ipse nihil omnino agat, inspirationem illam recipiens.*"

foundational work which was "in the beginning" of the Creator's way, which "was by him as a master workman" and was "daily his delight," as he marked out the foundations of the earth, and whose "delight was with the sons of men" (Prov. 8:1, 22, 30-31)? That mutual satisfaction of the wisdom of God in mankind, and of mankind in the wisdom of God, is the ground of our moral perception. But that is because the wisdom *in* creation is itself *of* creation. Too hasty a movement from the wisdom in creation to the divine Word can mislead us. For it is within the created world that the goods we love, the ends for which we act, the reasons we discover for each purpose we form, arise. It is not from within ourselves, certainly; it is not we that can confer the dignity of goods and ends on indifferent realities that chance throws across our path. But neither is it enough to say that God confers that dignity upon them. "Creation's being is God's pleasure," writes a theologian of our own time nobly, "creation's beauty God's glory; beauty reveals the shining of an uncreated light, a Taboric effulgence, upon all things, a *claritas* that discloses the lineaments of what it infuses and shows them to be the firm outlines of that weight, that *kabod*, that proclaims God's splendor."[22] And that is very fine; yet we must speak more explicitly of the location of this beauty. This is not the sunset splendor which, for a moment of poetic vision, "falls on castle walls." This splendor falls on no other site than where God has placed it, quite independently of our vision, the world he has made so sure that it cannot be moved, the unnegotiable form of our unformed agency, the school of our first and last purposes, the gazette that announces our enlistment in God's service.

Love of this ordered beauty, then, invites and implies knowledge of it. Just as a view of faith that is all cognition and not action is fundamentally defective, so is a view of love that is all action — an objectless goodwill towards anything and nothing. If faith stands on the boundary of knowledge, reaching out towards it, love occupies its heartlands; it dwells in a world of differentiated realities. We love any thing *as* some thing, which (with whatever qualifications we must attach to Butler's well-known apothegm) is "what it is and not some other thing." Loving knowledge is distinct and focused, attending to the quiddity and quality of its object. This coherence of emotion and cognition we may capture in the term "admiration," which is the knowledge of what can only be known in love, and the love of what can only be loved in knowledge. Admiration is not distinct

---

22. David Bentley Hart, *The Beauty of the Infinite* (Grand Rapids: Eerdmans, 2003), p. 252.

from love, nor a composite of love with something else, nor a subset of love, but simply love, so expounded as to show up the cognitive content always contained in it. It does not belong to subjective self-awareness before God, which is under the reign of faith. If love is allowed to slip backwards into the space that belongs to faith, we lose sight of its differentiated objectivity; it becomes an unworldly communication between the soul and God, that "flame of sacred love," which, as in Charles Wesley's beautiful hymn with more than a hint of gnosticism, "trembling to its source returns." Contemporary aesthetic metaphysics echoes this by giving priority among the aspects of love to *desire,* which attests the transcendence of the infinite by always exceeding the measure of its satisfaction. Without impugning that line of thought on its own terms, Ethics must pursue the question of love from quite another starting-point. Its initial contact with the infinite is not in yearning but in faith, and its initial engagement with love is not through "the beauty of the infinite" but the beauty of the finite. If desire's flight is ever to be well-aimed *action,* it must presuppose the comprehending gaze of admiration. But neither does admiration belong with deliberation, decision, and exertion, which are under the reign of hope. It is best described, perhaps, by Max Scheler's term, "moral cognition," which is explained as "fundamentally different from willing" and yet "the foundation for willing."[23]

To emphasize that love was wholly informed by knowledge was Augustine's greatest contribution to the Western understanding of love. Eastern Christianity had its own ways of recalling this truth, but for Augustine it was grounded in the doctrine of the Trinity: the Spirit, who is God *as* love, is consubstantial and coeternal with the Word through whom all things were made. It was this that encouraged him to mop up all the competing understandings of virtue in classical antiquity within the one overarching concept of love: prudence, temperance, fortitude, and justice were nothing else but love diversified by the demands of different circumstances.[24] The only true virtue was one that subordinated each experience, good and evil, to the love of God.[25] When he wrote that "my weight is my love, by which I am carried wherever I may be carried," the striking metaphor, conceiving weight as an attraction, underlined the objective focus of

---

23. Max Scheler, *Formalism in Ethics and Non-formal Ethics of Value,* trans. Manfred S. Frings and Roger L. Funk (Evanston: Northwestern University Press, 1973), p. 80.

24. Augustine, *De moribus ecclesiae,* 25.46.

25. Augustine, *City of God,* 19.4, 10.

love: it was not a power within us, an impulse driving us out into the world or up towards our supernatural destiny, but a purchase that objective reality had upon us.[26] "Weight," in a Trinitarian analogy of which Augustine was fond, represented the operation of the Holy Spirit in creation.[27] There was a vast difference, he held, between love ordered by reality and an evaluation based on merely subjective ends.[28]

Augustine was also a pioneer in giving pride of place in Ethics to Jesus' summary of the law as love of God and neighbor.[29] As the working of external goods upon us, love offered a framework in which the whole field of motivations could be ranged and the better distinguished from the less good. The coordination of the moral field under the head of love subjected every moral impulse to an integrative hermeneutic. This was the impact of monotheism upon practical reason, making possible an ordered and consistent morality by banishing the specter of unreconcilable claims that made nonsense of the agent's responsibility. The action of God himself became the highest and original object of love: "We love because he first loved us" (1 John 4:19). But all this had reference *to the moral field,* the worldly object of our admiration and attention. It did not replace the threefold structure of moral awareness. Love is a complement, not a rival, to the subjective disposition of faith, which "works through" love, and the temporal endurance of hope which is grounded in love. There is a proper pre-eminence of love over faith and hope, but love is never less and never more than the outworking of faith and the material of hope, the worldly reference that gives form to an agent answerable to God at a precise moment of time.

What is true of love is true also of the term Augustine used mainly as a synonym for it, "will." Augustine's "will" is neither a faculty of the mind nor an indeterminate power of self-assertion. It is either an act of resolution upon an end of action, or it is the object of that resolution, the thing willed. This was the classical sense of the word, in which the will was not a center of personal agency but an experience which the agent underwent.[30] The force of this is brought out clearly in a criticism of the Manichaeans, in which Au-

---

26. Augustine, *Confessions,* 13.9.10.

27. Referring to Wisdom 11:1: "By measure, number and weight thou didst order all things."

28. Augustine, *City of God,* 11.16.

29. See my remarks in *The Problem of Self-love in Saint Augustine* (New Haven: Yale University Press, 1980), p. 4.

30. In a passage of the *Tusculan Disputations* (4.6.12) which Augustine often discussed, Cicero identified *voluntas* as the rational agent's equivalent to a desire.

gustine reflected upon his own state of ambivalence before the conversion in the Milan garden: "Let them not say, when they perceive that in one man there are two wills at war with each other, that there is a conflict between two opposing minds, one good and one bad. . . . When there are so many appetible courses of action, the mind is torn by four or even more different wills."[31] Yet the term "will" could lead other thinkers in other directions. For Augustine's adversary Pelagius, inspired, perhaps, by Stoicism, the will was a sword which the saint would turn upon herself to slay herself in sacrifice.[32] The will as love, answering to created nature, or the will as personal assertion, turning against created nature? That was the civilizational choice that faced Christendom. In the course of the Middle Ages, by stages that are not well documented, the idea of will-against-nature, withdrawn from the world to become an immanent center of personal self-assertion, gained ground. Expressed in the monothelitism of the eighth century, it aroused the impassioned and costly resistance of Maximus Confessor, for whom the will must be something *a rational agent formed,* and so shaped by the "natural" conditions of that agent's existence, whether human, angelic, or divine. Peter and Paul willed "humanly," Michael and Gabriel "angelically"; they did not will "Peterwise," "Paulwise," "Michaelwise," and "Gabrielwise." The incarnate Son, as one person, willed *both* divinely *and* humanly.[33]

With the Stoic revival of the early Enlightenment the pinpoint agent-will of voluntarism, possessed of indeterminate energy and constructing its own forms of expression, came fully into its own in the West. There followed the collapse of the moral field: the structure of creation with its variety, order, and reflection of the Creator's glory no longer served to shape love and action, but the will became the exclusive giver of practical meaning. It no longer seemed to matter *in what* a will found satisfaction if it was consistently determined within itself, for as giver of meaning it must posit its own end. The climax of this development, reached at the end of the eighteenth century, was the opening sentence of Kant's *Grundlegung,* which, pretending merely to state the obvious, threw out a challenge only to be compared with the very similar opening motifs of his younger contemporary, Beethoven.

Late modern understandings of morality have been party to the col-

---

31. Augustine, *Confessions,* 8.10.24, trans. Philip Burton (London: Everyman, 2001).

32. Pelagius, *Epistula ad Demetriadem,* 1.1.

33. *Dialogus 7,* in *Maximus Confessor and His Companions: Documents from Exile,* ed. Pauline Allen and Bronwen Neil (Oxford: Oxford University Press, 2002), pp. 104-5.

lapse of the moral field in more than one way. On the one hand it is responsible for the persistent strain of ethical relativism and skepticism. Late moderns are easily cynical, viewing morality as a construction of that *ressentiment* which binds the weak together to contain the strong. On the other it accounts for the peculiarly innocent posture of much modern moral idealism, conflating its multitude of causes together into one grand but illusory project. The term "ethical," as used in such phrases as "ethical trade" and "ethical banking," covers many adventures in moral earnestness which have little in common with one another beyond the fact that the same good people support them through the same coffee mornings and the same sponsored bike rides. But that does not prevent them thinking they are serving one overarching end, spoken of as "saving the planet," "changing the world," or whatever. Reflective moral thought has different reasons for different moral judgments. If torture is to be opposed and organic farming supported, the grounds for the one are not the same as the grounds for the other. But the modern will, with its generalized high-mindedness, brushes the differences aside and conceals from itself that carbon-emissions, endemic poverty, torture, speculative bankers, and anti-immigration rallies pose diverse perils, and that saving the planet from one of them may not at all be conducive to saving it from the others.

Within the world of created and ordered goods God, too, is given to us to love. How can that be? The act of creation founds an analogy of good that corresponds to the analogy of being: God is "the good that makes good" (Ps. 119:68). Augustine's small essay *On the Nature of the Good* opens with the declaration, "The supreme good, than which none is greater, is God. As such it is the immutable good, which means it is truly eternal and truly immortal. All other goods are *from* this good, but not *of* this good. . . . If he alone is immutable, it follows that all he has made, and made out of nothing, is mutable."[34] The continuity of goodness is shown by tracing the source of created goods to the divine goodness itself. It is not simply that God is good in one way, creatures in another. The good of the creator stands in relation to the good of the creature not as in parallel but in sequence. God's goodness is goodness "itself," or good "supremely," and the application of the epithet "good" to any creature is possible only because that creature has, as such, a relation to God. Created good is a kind of God-relatedness, a reference to an original that lies beyond itself.

Love of good, too, is a relation to the good. What I find, in admiration,

---

34. *De natura boni*, 1.

to be good, I find to be good *for me.* That "for me" follows necessarily from my admiration; if I could not say "good for me," I could not say "good" at all. Far from narrowing my view of the good to the scope of a purely selfish interest, the sense of my own relation to the good broadens my view of what my interest consists in. I myself belong to the world in which the good is good; I, too, am indebted to the goodness of the good; I cannot pose as an impartial judge of it. And from this appreciation of my love of what is good, there is born gratitude, an existential self-acknowledgment in the experience of the good. An ex-Catholic businessman wrote, contemplating the success of his enterprises, "Si je croyais en Dieu, je lui dirais merci"! It is hard not to feel pity for his dilemma. For gratitude identifies good as a communication directed towards me, so that to grasp the good, I must know from what source it comes. Once I catch myself being grateful, I close off the possibility of thinking of the good simply as a comfortable surface I have happened to brush up against. It has becomes a disclosure. The poet of the fourth Psalm heard his despairing contemporaries ask, "Who will show us any good?" (Ps. 4:6). But what if the good has somehow been shown us? Must we not turn to its source, and address it: "Lift up the light of your face upon us!"? After the death of his wife John Donne wrote:[35]

> Since shee whom I lov'd hath payd her last debt
> To nature and to hers, and my good is dead,
> And her soule early into heaven ravished,
> Wholly on heavenly things my mind is sett.
> Here the admyring her my mind did whett
> To seeke thee, God; so streames do shew their head.

To her husband Ann Donne was "my good," and since, not being a possessive individualist, he understood the logic of that expression, he knew that it raised the question of a "head" from which the "stream" of good had flowed towards him.

To this movement of thought upwards to a First Good there is a corresponding descent. As we cannot interrogate the idea of objective goodness without reference to a First Good, so divine goodness is an idea we cannot think through without reference to the goods of creation. We must say, of course, that God is good "in himself," not only good by virtue of his good

---

35. *The Divine Poems,* ed. Helen Gardner (Oxford: Oxford University Press, 1952, 2001), p. 14. The Jacobean spelling of the word "hearse" has caused puzzlement to some readers.

communications to us. But that predication, like the statement that God exists before time, is made anagogically. It would be as preposterous to suppose that we could grasp the content of God's goodness apart from the communication of creaturely goods as it would be to suppose we could comprehend his pre-eternity without leaning on the crutches of a notion of time. Loving God "above all things," then, leads back to loving created goods, but it does so in a specific way and in a specific order and under specific controls. To love God, as to love any other being, we must find language to convey our disposition, objects to serve as gifts, contexts and purposes to provide for significant co-presence. Love requires its communicative medium of loveliness. Love of God is affirmed in and through our other loves, structuring them and ordering them, so that with each new discovery of good that world and time lay open to us, the question of the love of God is put again, its sovereignty over other loves reasserted or forgotten. For love of the world and of the God who gives the world occupies our experience not as a settled condition, but as a series of openings and adventures.

Hope and the Future

"Today if you will hear his voice . . . !": the dramatic disruption in the middle of the song of praise in Psalm 95 warns us that admiration and worship of the good things God has made, even of God as their maker and protector, cannot be the end of our response. We have been summoned to sing, rejoice, and give thanks for the great king above all gods, for the hand which holds the depths and height of the earth together, for the sea and dry land which attest his authorship, and for the human race protected and guided as a flock by its shepherd. And at that point we are confronted with something quite different: a unique moment of time, "today," with a unique danger, "harden not your hearts!" The greatest commentator on the ancient poem, the author of the Letter to the Hebrews, seizes (4:6-11) upon the disruptive moment in the text: "*Again* he appoints a certain day, 'Today!'" It is held open to us. "It remains for some to enter. . . . we must strive . . . !" Not a closed point in past history, but not divorced from history, either, for in order to comprehend this new "today" as we meet it, we have to learn to see it against the background of those past todays which it resembles: "harden not your hearts, as in the day of temptation."

In the moment that is given us, then, we meet the challenge of moving from the world into future time. Agency is not realized in admiration and love of wisdom, but in action. But action requires thought about the character of the moment. A complex proverb given us by Qoheleth (Eccles. 8:5ff.) draws out the paradoxical aspect of this movement: "One who keeps a commandment knows no evil thing, and the heart of a wise man knows time and judgment." But is not knowing time and judgment knowing an evil thing? "For to every purpose there is a time and judgment, for great is the evil of man upon him. For he is not one who knows what shall be, for how it shall be, who shall tell him?"[36] The proverb describes a paradox: the law-abiding man who has no evil in his mind must be the wise man who has "time and judgment" in his mind (i.e., "knowing how to discern the right moment"), precisely in order to respond to an evil which always threatens to overwhelm him. The *innocence* of the gaze which bows before the lovely order of a law-governed world becomes, without being lost, the *cunning* of a practical discernment that negotiates peril at every turn, having no view of the remote future. We are reminded of Jesus' command: "Be as clever as serpents and as innocent as doves!" (Matt. 10:16). There is a necessary progress of moral thought from the simplicity of admiration to deliberative complexity. Both the proverb and Jesus' summary of it warn against false innocence, an imagination that one can carry on existence by loving the good and ignoring practical demands. They also warn against a false sophistication, which, determined not to evade the actualities, loses its purchase on the vision of God's order. It is precisely as a *keeper of the law* that one can be wise in knowing when a decision is required.

To face our time actively is always to face in one direction, the future. It is not an empty habit of speech when we refer to a major deliberative question (for instance, projected constitutional change in Scotland) as

36. Current English Bible translations give the reader a hard time with this proverb, some refusing even to treat it as a single unit. The version I have given is literal, but quite comprehensible. The points at which interpretative differences have arisen are, briefly: (i) the imperfect tenses for the verb "know" are often understood as having a future sense, but it is clearer to treat them as a continuous present; (ii) "judgment" *(mishpat)* is subjected to a variety of paraphrases by versions that do not appreciate the hendiadys; (iii) "purpose" is *hephetz,* "delight," which in Ecclesiastes has the sense of "project" or "practical affair"; the idea of "delight" need not be excluded, but "matter" on its own will not suffice; (iv) *kî,* meaning "for," occurs four times in quick succession. To translate just one of these as "although" is a rather desperate expedient. Behind this there lies a common interpretative assumption that Qoheleth does not agree with the traditional view of wisdom and intends to contradict it, yet the more positive reading is supported directly by 3:1. I am grateful to David Reimer for pointing this out to me and for drawing attention to the important parallels between this saying and the preceding one (8:2-4).

"the future of Scotland." Nor is it misleading that we praise successful deliberation as "prudence," i.e., *pro-videntia* or "foresight." The present has no duration of its own; the "here and now" is a mathematical point, constituted and contained by what Heidegger has taught us to call its "horizons" of past and future, reception of experience on the one side opening up a view of some possible self-actualization on the other. Action requires a future at the very margin of the present like a boat lying at the quay, ready to be stepped into and pushed off. The future is not, like the past, a unified and coherent whole, a single web of history spread out. Future time is not yet reduced to the sequential order and factual univocity of history, but is envisaged only in fragmentary and elusive ways. The world has its future, which we cannot anticipate at all; there are futures we can anticipate, by prediction on the basis of observed regularities or by seizing on possibilities in fear or desire; there is an absolute future of God's purpose, given in promise; and there is an immediate future into which we may project action. The reason, we are told, why knowing time and judgment are necessary to any purpose is that "he is not one who knows what shall be."

For simplicity's sake we may speak of the many futures in terms of two types of perception: "anticipation" founded on the present, and "hope" founded on promise. Anticipation teases out a future that lurks within the present as a possibility. Look at a rose bush on which some yellow flowers have opened, others are still in green bud, others still retain the shape of the bud though the envelope has fallen away to reveal the color of the petals. If you saw only what was actually the case as you looked, you would see three different kinds of flower, one spreading, golden and fragrant, another green and tight as a nut, a third nut-shaped but yellow. But we know enough of rose bushes to know that they are the same kind of flower at different stages of growth. We know how a rose typically grows, and that is enough. We need no definite information about the past or future of *this* bush or *this* bud, only a familiarity with the temporal form, the patterns of becoming, growing, and dying that are specific to roses. The perception of temporal form holds actual and un-actual states before the mind together — a perception not given by any of the five senses directly, but relying on the capacity to remember and generalize, yet still a perception, similar to the ability to see three-dimensional objects when only one plane is on view at any given moment.[37] On the basis of such perception we reasonably,

---

37. For this discussion see especially Jean-Yves Lacoste, "La Phénomenalité de l'Anticipation," in *La Phénominalité de Dieu* (Paris: Cerf, 2008).

though without certainty, anticipate outcomes: the buds will open, or perhaps they will be nipped by a late frost.

Desire and fear, the two emotions relating to the future, are passionate anticipations. Because they are passionate, they have an effect not only on how we experience the world, but also on how we exert ourselves in it. David Hume was the first of the moderns to propose that the passionate-reactive effect could provide a sufficient account of the rationality of human action. Reason conceived as the "slave of the passions" was, in effect, a downgrading of deliberation. Thought was concerned only to design active means to satisfy dominant fears or desires. "Right" could be dissolved into "good" in one direction and into "must" in the other. But this was to lay too great a practical weight on anticipation. Desire as such projects no action, but simply, as it were, catches sight of the possible peeping round the edges of the actual. There are hopeless desires, as there are paralyzing fears, which never point a way to action. And there are alternative desires or fears which we entertain simultaneously, each capable of satisfaction in isolation but not all together. Desire is speculative; its impotence is not an accident. Sometimes we think of desire as an underdeveloped exertion of will, a resolution lacking sufficient muscle, a "wish," or (in Jonathan Edwards' pleasing expression) a "weak woulding." From which we may conclude (disastrously) that effective agency depends on our whipping desire and fear into a furious froth. But agency is brought to effect not by desire but by hope. Hope is not a heightened form of anticipation. It responds to promise, presumes on a future that is absolute. If, like desire, hope terminated in the thought of pleasant futures lurking as possibilities within present states of affairs, it could not be a virtue. Mr. Micawber is not virtuous; the dreamer of a world where no one goes to bed hungry is not virtuous. Hope differs from desire because it attends to a different future, the future of God's promise.

Promise speaks of what is far beyond the horizon of anticipation. The assurances it offers are not to be had on the basis of the present. Its future is remote, "new" as no extrapolation of temporal form can be new. It offers no speculative outline, no clearer anticipation that could underwrite a rational unfolding of immanent possibilities — a new age of mission, a more deeply Christian civilization, an ecumenical convergence of the great religious families of the earth, a juster political order, or whatever. Imperspicuous in every respect except in the finality of its justice, the promise threatens us, to the extent that we rely on anticipations, with nothing but disappointment and frustration. Yet in denying us the speculative assurance we crave for, promise allows hope to be born, and through hope opens the way to agency. "We walk by faith and not by sight" (2 Cor. 5:7). How can faith, "seeking understanding" as it always must, direct its walk into the darkness of the future? It can do so through hope, which is, to recall the famous mixed metaphor of the Epistle to the Hebrews, "the anchor within the veil" (Heb. 6:19), the one thing that is firm in a future of obscurity. It enables us to face uncertainty in the certain knowledge that whatever the future holds, it holds the coming of the Son of Man.

For all that it denies us speculative certainty, the promised future interests us existentially as agents. For its effect is to bring into focus our view of the immediately possible, the space where purposeful action is now offered us. It presents us with a boat for our initiative to step into, a boat to push off from the quay and to pull upon with our oars. No longer allowed to suppose that the next thing will follow from the last, or that what we do next does not matter, we find ourselves shockingly summoned from imaginative anticipations into practical readiness. In presenting us with the certainty of the world's last end, hope clears a space of freedom before our feet, even if that space is no larger than will allow for a disciplined and patient waiting. The object of hope, the apostle reminds us, is what we do not see (Rom. 8:24). I hope for what I cannot anticipate, for deep changes in the world which can come about when the lion shall lie down with the lamb. Does hope imply total darkness, then, the complete absence of knowledge? No, but it is the severest purgation of our knowledge, reduced from the diffused daylight of the world to the narrow shaft of light that connects God's future to our own, the remote to the near, the object of the promise to the step before us. It is not, of course, that wider knowledge of the world is irrelevant to deliberation, for only with a clear view of where we stand and what stands near us can we begin to deliberate at all. But as we carry through our deliberation that clear view of the context recedes into the surrounding shadows and our attention closes in upon the "good works . . . prepared before us to walk in" (Eph. 2:10), right before our feet, that is, where the light source from beyond the known world falls, summoning us to witness to the promise in our action. The moment of action is also the moment of temptation, when our settled perceptions of the world and ourselves may fail us. Only hope suffices to address it.

And so, the apostle continues, if we hope, we also expect and endure (Rom. 8:25). Within the net of predictable anticipations this space is cleared for us, not a yawning vacancy, but sufficient room, however narrow, to give effect to our agency. Discerning the space is that work of thought spoken of by Qoheleth as "judgment" and known to us commonly as "deliberation." Without the promise we could not deliberate, for nothing could assure us that an exertion of our own could constitute a "work" that might count for good in eternity. Hope allows us to discern it, and so to form a purpose, in which the immediate space of our action is aligned with the ultimate goal of God's purposes. Augustine, reading Saint Paul's words about his ambition, "forgetting what lies behind and straining forward to what lies ahead, I press on toward the goal" (Phil. 3:13-14), seized on two verbs in his Latin translation, *intendere* and *extendere*. We may be "intent," he concluded, on what lies ahead for us only if we are "extended" to the future that is ultimately to come into being.[38] The alignment of the two objects, the near and the far, is not that of a means to an end — not, at any rate, as we normally understand those terms. No act of ours can be a condition for the coming of God's Kingdom. God's Kingdom, on the contrary, is the condition for our acting; it underwrites the intelligibility of our purposes. Our action may be framed consistently with it; it may acquire its immediate purpose from the eternal purpose that it foreshadows, indirectly but patiently.

Work and Rest

And should we not stop there? Can our view go further than where hope has narrowed the width of love down to the "one thing needful"? But action cannot terminate in a leap into empty space. It must have an "end," foreseen in the logic of the act's conception, effected in the logic of the act's completion. Evoked in the first place by promise, action would not achieve itself if it never proved the promise in its effect, but merely followed it, as though chasing a will o' the wisp, from one imagined future to another.

If we attend carefully to the context of Paul's assertion that "the greatest of these is love" (1 Cor. 13:13), we can hardly fail to be struck by two dominant interests that have framed it. One is the interest in social cooperation, and on that we shall postpone extended reflection to the explorations of a later volume. The other, to which we shall attend here, is the interest in finality. Prophecies, knowledge, tongues, the apostle insists, shall pass away like children's games, because their function can be exhausted. The triad of faith, hope, and love, on the other hand, has a permanence surviving every passing form that human action may take. To call love

38. Augustine, *In Epistulam Iohannis*, 4.6.

"greatest" does not mean that the triadic structure of practical thought has been left behind. It is not the ultimate vindication of quietism, not a summons to feeling and vision without energy and purpose, the melting away of the sharp edges of initiative into the soft curves of perception. It asserts the ordering of human action, with its distinctive triadic structure, to accomplishment. Yet the accomplishment recalls the central moment, that of love, and subsumes the other two moments under it. Love is action's mode of participating in eternity.[39]

How so? The contribution of love to action lay in its *objectivity*. It was to this that those who wished to purify love of self-concern were pointing: in love, affect is wholly absorbed in its object, which is to say, wholly taken up into knowledge. Love is the reflective moment of practical reason turned outwards to reality, taking stock of the good that is objectively given, including its own relation to what is given. Love's final preeminence means that reflection is not *expended,* and so *superseded,* in becoming the ground from which we proceed to act. On the contrary, as hope bears its fruit in action, action performed feeds back into love's reflection. The relation to the real world forged by love is irreversible, and through action continually strengthens itself. As moral reason passes from faith to love and on through hope into action, so it must finally pass back to love again. This is how, reflecting on its own performance, moral *reason* was subsumed into moral *teaching,* and moral *teaching* into moral *theory* — a reflective step in each case, but without losing the active commitment which gave rise to it.

We may set aside, then, interpretations of the primacy of love which conceive it as a foundational subjective motivation, an original practical impetus behind categorical practical judgments, such as Gérard Gilleman's theory of love as the *tendance foncière,* "the substance of revealed morality, not a chapter."[40] This confuses the sovereignty of love with the antecedence of faith; it collapses the triad of faith, love, and hope into a monadic reign of "love" — though it is not in fact love, since it is not objective; it is only the modern "will." Liberal Protestant thinkers of the twentieth century, too, found this account attractive. "Love, and do as you will!" seemed to some to be the charter of anti-legalism.[41] Of the many reasons for re-

39. For Augustine's carefully balanced statement on this, see *De doctrina Christiana,* 1.37.41ff.

40. Gérard Gilleman, *Le Primat de la Charité en Théologie Morale* (Brussels: Édition Universelle; Paris: Desclée de Brouwer, 1952), p. 3.

41. For the canonization of this remark from Augustine's *In Epistulam Iohannis,* 7.8, see, notoriously, Joseph Fletcher, *Situation Ethics* (London: SCM, 1965).

jecting this idea one is decisive: by treating love as an original motivation it deprives it of categorical content, which means that it allows any and every categorical content we may wish to foist upon it. It does nothing, therefore, to direct our steps, a consequence embraced with equal candor by Joseph Fletcher and Joseph Fuchs, S.J.[42] In classical Augustinian doctrine the two-fold love-command presided over other judgments not by being the distillation of original motivation, but by commanding the love *of God and neighbor*. It offered the key to the moral ordering of the world, not to the subjective motions of the soul.

On similar grounds we reject the concept of love as a primitive dynamic capable of constituting its own reality around it, not least the famous concept of agape, "creating value in its object," to which Anders Nygren gave currency some eighty years ago. Love was to be a "fundamental motif," a founding conception, an evangelical metaphysic of morals.[43] Differing from the motivational idea in recognizing a definite alternative to agape, Nygren's conception was a child of the post-Kantian fascination with plural worldviews. Agape was a world-descriptive matrix, which turned the world as eros perceived it on its head, accomplishing a Nietzschean transvaluation of values. Agape was not wholly uncategorical, for it told a story about the world which could intelligibly be contradicted, but its categories were not the categories of human life in the world, but only of the alterity of the divine. For that reason, though it did not displace faith, which was still the proper subjective response to God's love, it did away with hope entirely.

In one respect, however, Nygren guided us correctly. We shall understand the primacy of love more clearly if we start, with him, from the assertion of Saint John that "God is love" (1 John 4:16). "Is," rather than "attains," "practices," or even "becomes." Of God alone can it be said that his love needs no faith to afford a competent subject for it, no hope to carry it forward into action. God's love is its own subject, its own enactment. In God there is no distinction between apprehension and comprehension, between admiration and decision, for to be and to love and to act are one and the same in him. The God who is love rests in his own activity. In that respect God is not as we are; "love" can be predicated of God and man not

42. Joseph Fuchs, *Christian Morality: The Word Becomes Flesh* (Dublin: Gill and Macmillan; Washington, DC: Georgetown University Press, 1981).

43. Anders Nygren, *Agape and Eros*, trans. Philip S. Watson (New York: Harper & Row, 1969), p. 210.

univocally, but only by analogy. The love-monism which substituted itself for the threefold moral foundation of the Christian life expressed an age-old yearning for a divine humanity. Monophysitism, in celebrating the Incarnation as the coming-to-be of "one nature of the enfleshed Logos," gave early expression to the mythic history of theandric union, and in claiming for that one nature a unique ordering of will, it revealed the practical pretensions of its myth. The flower which grew from that seed we have seen in technological post-humanism: man willing as God, giving being to all that his mind conceives, and finally repeating (on a higher level) God's accomplishment of giving birth to a yet more perfect being than himself. But if this thrusting of man into God's place lay at the heart of a false understanding of love, there is also a right understanding, not only of love itself but also of mankind's calling into the presence of God. The saying "he became man that we might become God" was not first uttered with monophysite intent.[44] There is a true "partaking of the divine nature" (2 Peter 1:4) to be spoken of, an entry into the rest of the God who is love, held out before mankind as its supernatural end.

Any knowledge of what we do at the moment we undertake to do it is limited to our own practical purposes. We say someone "knows what he is doing" when he is clear about what he is "up to." What he is *really* doing he may not know at all. In the purposing of action the scope of love's knowledge is narrowed to the future before our feet, and even that is "known" only in a fragile and hypothetical way. For action to attain its end it must recover an objective knowledge of itself. Reflective conduct is reflection *after*, not only *before* acting. Not to know what we *have* done is to fail to bring action to accomplishment, which is one way we may fail as agents altogether. But in recovering objective knowledge of our action we loosen our exclusive hold on it. It is now no longer simply *our* duty, *our* project, but a deed that God has done in the world through us, a mercy vouchsafed us — as Cromwell liked to describe his military victories, too complacently, perhaps, but by no means wrongly. The completed work is still "ours" in that we can know ourselves reflectively in it, but it is "God's" in that we receive it back from him as a gift. As the world in which I undertook to act was an object of grateful love, so now my act has taken its place in that world, also an object of gratitude and even admiration — "I am a wonder to myself!" as John Wesley exclaimed. That God should have allowed me to do *this* thing, whatever it is — bring up a child, perhaps, or

---

44. Athanasius, *De incarnatione verbi*, 54.

care for an invalid, or design a clever piece of computer software — achieves an objectivity, at last, which allows for a wonder that is not mere pride or self-love. Love's sovereignty lies in its reflective power to subsume our action into the intelligible whole of God's world.

In this reflective reflux of active engagement we can see how the bare idea of "action" is articulated into "rest" and "work." "Rest" is the completion of action. It is not simply a reversion from action to reflection, a final victory of contemplation over exertion. One may reflect on things one has not done, but only in reflecting on what one *has* done can one rest. In reflection on action our agency is still in play; the action remains "ours," the engagement which has given worldly reality to our agency. What has changed is simply the relaxation of care and striving. In Jewish and Christian moral thought the sabbath was a sign of work's accomplishment. "God saw all that he had made, and it was good" (Gen. 1:31). In blessing the sabbath God extended to mankind his glad rest in his accomplishment, that we, too, might rest in accomplishment. Our intelligent nature is satisfied in action to the extent that it enters God's blessing. Correspondingly, it is only in the light of rest that we can think of action as work. Activity may have many different qualifications, as hateful servitude or free initiative, as slavish imitation or high artistry, as destruction or creation, as obsessive meddling or attentive care. It attains the dignity of work only as it reaches the point of completion. "The end crowns the work," as the proverb has it. As completed work our agency has a place within the world, and can be offered back to God in praise as the contribution to the world's preservation and redemption which he has been pleased to accomplish through us.

For it is in praise that we enter God's rest, both within the ordinary weekly rhythm of work and rest and within history as a whole, which culminates, as we are taught to hope, in eternal praise. But praise is also, by its very nature, a publication. Praise of God makes his works the content of a communication among his creatures. And so our own works, constituted first as an offering of praise to God, are constituted secondly as a contribution to the common world we share with our fellow-creatures. It is tempting to concentrate on this second aspect of work at the expense of the first. Action becomes work, we may say, if and as it is a useful service to other people. We distinguish work from recreation not by what we do or how good we are at it, nor even by how much time we spend on it, but by how much others depend on our doing it. The hobby chef can earn a *cordon bleu* like any professional, but the professional must be at the restaurant for his clients, come rain come shine. This interpretation of work as social function puts second things in first place. That in blessing our actions as work God will bless them to others' use, too, is true. It is because God blesses it that we may make it a communication. But the social character of work does not arise from its usefulness; its usefulness arises from its social character. The attempt to derive the sociality of work from utility breaks work down into a market of fragmentary operations, in which nothing can be done on its own terms and for its own sake, but everything becomes what someone else wants to make of it. If it is "useful" to the manufacture of cars that one operator should do nothing but tighten bolts, another nothing but test tire pressure, that does not make those operations good work. That they cannot be, for they are not enough to satisfy the intelligent nature of those who perform them. And if they cannot be good work, how can they fulfill the social task of cooperation? The paradigm case of work that resists the criterion of utility is the work of art — especially the disturbing and inaccessible one. Whether or not the public will take pleasure in it, and will pay to see or hear or read it, the artist must stand to the severe canons of the art. The choreographer at whose ballet I found myself closing my eyes can hardly have had it in mind to cause *me* pleasure! No doubt he thought that if those wriggles and jumps could be got as near as possible to the way God conceived them, my own bored incomprehension might be illumined in due time. And that is what, as an artist, he ought to have thought. What would the balletic art be, after all, if it depended on the tastes of people like me? The artist is answerable to God for making one species of work as good as it can be made. Scholars distracted by the buzz of "impact" should remember that their case is no different.

In the simplest example, that of an act of making or production, the completion of a work precedes its acquisition of a reflective social character in a simple temporal sequence. Before I can publish this book, I must finish writing it. When I have finished it and published it, it will still be my book, but the manner of my ownership of it will have changed, for it will no longer be the project that I brood over in my unsociable hours and retreat into the solitude of my study to pursue; it will be something I can handle as others do, and can discuss as others discuss. But if we take a more complex task, that of a parent bringing up children, the transition from project to accomplishment is not focused on a decisive moment. There will be a day, no doubt, when the children are self-supporting adults, when the parent, no longer responsible for turning them out neatly and controlling their behavior, can simply take pride in them as members of society. But long before that, while the parental labor still continues, there

are incremental moments of accomplishment and satisfaction: the performance in the nativity play, the arrival of the school report, cheering the
losing side in the match, and so on. Parents are always rehearsing, one
might say, for an accomplishment that will never *quite* be achieved this
side of the grave. And in this respect they are a better model for accomplishment than the craftsman or the author, for they illustrate how at the
point of rest, even more than in the heat of exertion, there is ownership.
While their children objectify what God has done through their labor of
parenthood, and done for the world and not only for them, they are still
their parents' children, their presence in the world still necessarily, though
at one remove, their parents' presence. To use a classical theological term,
the parent has "enjoyment" of them.

At the heart of eschatology is the promise that we all must appear before
God to be judged according to our works. Our deeds are to be events in history, subject to ultimate appraisal. Not a mere estimate such as a reviewer
might offer on a published book, leaving the work itself just as it was, quite as
likely to make the reviewer look foolish as the reviewer the book. True judgment is an effective act. It discloses and confirms the significance of our
works, bringing them to their decisive appearance. Until in the end we have
brought our lives to God's view, we cannot complete them.[45] Rest, which en-
joys the blessing of God, can be entered as we contemplate God's works with
him and see them as he does. Satisfaction needs its object, something real to
repose upon; our own works, our lives, do not possess that objectivity when
they are kept to ourselves. Their true value is as an element in a larger plan.
So long as we live, a shift in the light can persuade us that our life and work
are pointless; great souls (Aquinas and Grotius among them) have enter-
tained on their deathbeds the fearful suspicion that their labor has
amounted to nothing but a vanity of vanities. Work is the pane of glass
through which, as Herbert understood, we may "passe and then the heav'n
espie."[46] To espy heaven is to see our life and work within the purposes of
God, a contribution which, of grace, he has permitted our agency to make to
his universal plan. As John Donne put it, taking up the proverb:

45. Jean-Yves Lacoste, *Être en Danger* (Paris: Cerf, 2011), p. 181, in criticism of what he
sees as Heidegger's tendency to talk about existence-towards-death as though "from beyond
the grave": "*Le dernier mot appartient à l'inachevé. . . . Nous ne pouvons, non plus, dans
l'horizon de la mort, spéculer sur un accomplissement que rien ne nous permet de décrire.*"
46. George Herbert, "The Elixir," in *The Works of George Herbert*, ed. F. E. Hutchinson
(Oxford: Clarendon, 1941), p. 184.

The ends crown our works, but thou crown'st our ends,
For at our end begins our endless rest.[47]

Is there in this train of thought, we may worry, a diversion of eschatology to become a mere teleology, a symbolic representation of what it is that we look forward to achieving when we act? The worry is not entirely foolish. Ethics cannot speak directly to eschatology; that sphere of discourse is the prerogative of Dogmatics, assisted, perhaps, but not led by Philosophy. Reflection on human action can tell us nothing about the content of the promise and the end of history. Yet Ethics can and must speak *out of* eschatology, having heard Dogmatics and Philosophy on the matter. It can treat eschatology with respect as a discourse, to which it cannot contribute, that is really and truly *about* the end of history. It does not need to reduce it to an imaginative projection upon the heavens of the ordinary earthly routine of human activity. Jewish and Christian theologians received a narrative of creation in which the sabbath, the crown of each week, was understood first and foremost as an accomplishment of creation. Rest was presented in this narrative as an immanent this-worldly phenomenon, an ordinance for the marking of routine time which could illumine from within the meaning of worldly time as the creaturely work of God. But they found they could not think of it solely within those terms. The shaping of time by weeks could not, like the sequence of days and nights or even the monthly cycles of the moon, speak for itself as a given feature of nature; it had the character of an imposition. Its significance lay in the sphere of history. Once given the concept of history, the significance of the weekly rest became clearer: it pointed forward to a final achievement. The promise of a sabbath rest for all endeavor is a precondition for thinking of history at all. But that means it is a precondition for thinking of Ethics, too, for Ethics is framed by history and is always forming moral concepts to address history. It does so whenever we ask about the ultimate direction and purpose of our lives, or about the purpose of institutions and enterprises that can only mature after our deaths. If eschatology is no more than a myth of human action, no less mythical are the moral concepts of a life realized successfully as a whole from youth to age, or of service rendered to future generations. Any hint of illusoriness about the end of history immediately infects the intermediate ends we believe in and work towards. From the final resting place the logic of interim resting

47. John Donne, "La Corona."

places flows backwards into history, and gives history its rhythm and point. Ethics, with nothing to say directly about the final resting place, can point us to these interim places. It can speak of provisional accomplishments granted to worldly undertakings, and not least of the accomplishment of communication, which turns work into cooperation, facilitating the work of other agents. Creation and eschatology, when well focused, illumine each other.

And here we return to the point from which we set out, "justification." At the end as at the beginning, we are justified by the free grace of God. "By faith," in that our agency is summoned to exist by his gift and not by immanent energy or purpose. "Not of works," in that the sum of all our actions cannot amount to an accomplishment that commands his blessing. The noun in that phrase is plural: to speak of "works" is to speak of the multiple effects I produce by my constant activity. But if we were to keep to the singular, we might go so far as to say that the end of my existence in the world is, as such, my "work," and that nothing could possibly justify me before God other than *this* work, since justification is precisely the acceptance God extends to my active being. But — and this is why the no-entry sign is so important — no amount of initiative, exertion, performance, and abstention, conceived, carried through, wrapped up and packed off to the general admiration of the watching crowds, could ever comprise that acceptable contribution to the world, the "work" which God expects and demands of me. The work I have in hand is nothing less than myself, and to all those multiple activities the question will have to be put whether they make of me the being God would make of me, and the answer will have to be given: no, of themselves they can make nothing like that. Only as God blesses those multiple activities, lends them a point and a coherence they lack otherwise and makes them acceptable to himself, do they become that "work" with which he is graciously pleased because from first to last it has been *his* work. All this without speaking (yet) of sin and misdoing, of wrong that cannot be made good — things which must certainly be spoken about, too, in their due place, which is neither the first nor the last place, incidentally, but a place in the middle between them. "Justification by faith and not by works" is a theme only brought to full expression when it speaks of Christ as redeemer and restorer of a broken and sinful humanity. Yet when it is brought to that expression there is nothing so very unheard-of about it, since Christ is the Word who gives intelligibility to whatever comes to be. The redemption and restoration of sinful mankind sharpens the dependence that is already the deepest truth about our works:

they are whatever they are out of the providential dispositions of God's goodness. Abel and Cain both offered of the produce of their work. God judged their offerings differently. What more can possibly be said?

By the dogmatic theologian, indeed, pressing back to the causes of things, no more. Behind the sovereignty of God there is nowhere further back to go. But Ethics has a journey in the opposite direction to make, a return into the foreground of our action. God's negative judgment, as the narrative has it, was not the end of Cain, but a new beginning: it posed the challenge, "If you do well, will you not be accepted? And if you do not do well, sin is crouching at the door" (Gen. 4:7). Even after the murder of his brother there remained for Cain the life of the city, huddled for defense together with his perpetually procreating and brawling sons and grandsons with their tents, animals, metalwork, and bagpipes. Ethics reflects upon the reasoning of men and women who still live under that "mark" which protects the race of murderers in its sad alienation, who pray and act in response to the still valid promise, "If you do well . . ." and the still valid warning, "If you do not do well. . . ." It can reflect on moments that verify that promise and warning, moments of achievement and moments of failure, and yet it does so in the service of those who have time and judgment before them, and may still act. How long is that time? How final is that judgment? Ah! that is something that Ethics cannot tell, but only that time is given, and judgment must follow!

Index of Names and Subjects

Index of Names and Subjects

Index of Scripture References